MW01139658

ISLAND OF THE INNOCENT

A Consideration of the Book of Job

DIANE GLANCY

TURTLE POINT PRESS *Brooklyn, New York*

Requests for permission to make copies of any part of the work should be sent to:
Turtle Point Press, 208 Java Street, Fifth Floor, Brooklyn, NY 11222
info@turtlepointpress.com

Library of Congress Control Number: 2020932735
Cataloging-in-Publication Data is available from the publisher upon request.

Design by Alban Fischer Design

ISBN: 978-1-885983-80-0

Printed in the United States of America

The title of this book only appears in the King James Version of the Bible— When men are cast down, then you shall say, There is a lifting up, and he shall save the humble person. He shall deliver the island of the innocent: and it is delivered by the pureness of your hands— JOB 22:29-30 KJV.

This is the Revised Standard Version— For God abases the proud, but he saves the lowly. He delivers the innocent man, you will be delivered through the cleanness of your hands— JOB 22:29-30 RSV.

I like the wobbliness of translations. The instability of something there when viewed in a certain way, and not there when viewed in another. I like the other uncertainties— Who has clean hands when even pride was found in the upright Job? And where is the island of the innocent?

CONTENTS

PART ONE

I wanted to explore the Book of Job with poems and poetic prose until the fissures appeared. Other times and places bled into the story. Among the first to disrupt the text were the Indians and the history of America. Feathers appeared over the ridge of a hill. The feathers were in headdresses. The headdresses were on heads. The Indians were foreign to the story of Job, as far as it had been understood. But— if ever there was trial and suffering, 6,000 years didn't matter. The Indians could step back. Job could step forward— current to whatever circumstance there is.

MAY LIT THE SKY.

His canoes unfastened. Hay rolls unrolled. Sabeans, three bands of Chaldeans, fire, and whirlwind take seven sons and three daughters, the flocks and herds— sheep, camels, asses, and oxen. Three friends and a fourth come from their own places to talk about the reasons for suffering. Blaming Job of wrongdoing but, as it turns out— it is a trial from our God, the lovely one, who taunts Satan— have you considered my servant Job?[1]— Now there was a day when the sons of God came to present themselves before the Lord. This is interesting enough.

Was it innocence Job had known? Not Latin *in* [not] *nocere* [to hurt]. He was not hurting others. But he himself was hurt.

---

[1] JOB 1:8

1

DORMER

I don't care about trouble.
I care about trouble more than anything.
The boy hits a ball.
Despite all evidence to the contrary.
Suffering is true.
It is wise.
It opens a house you never knew was there.
Or a part of the house you never knew was there.
Though you always dreamed there was another story to the house.
One above the second floor.
It was there when you slept.
The boy in the yard with his bat.
At night a universe full of white balls.

A TREATISE ON SUFFERING IN UZ

And Satan came among them. And the Lord said to Satan, whence comest thou? Then Satan answered the Lord, and said, From going to and fro in the earth, and from walking up and down in it. And the Lord said to Satan, Hast thou considered my servant Job, that there is none like him in the earth, a perfect and upright man, one that feareth God, and escheweth evil? Then Satan answered the Lord, and said, Doth Job fear God for naught? Hast not thou made an hedge about him, and about his house, and about all that he hath on every side? Thou has blessed the work of his hands, and his substance is increased in the land. But put forth thine hand now, and touch all that he hath, and he will curse thee to thy face. And the Lord said unto Satan, Behold, all that he hath is in thy power; only upon himself put not forth thine hand. So Satan went forth from the presence of the Lord— JOB 1:6–12*

Give us this day our daily understanding.
Lead us not into thinking
God brags and brings big trouble to his servant Job
blindsided by the loss of his beloved sons and daughters, his herds
and flocks,
[7000 sheep, 3000 camels, 500 yoke of oxen, 500 she asses]
his friends who visit with accusations it is his fault after all
and what has he been doing to bring upon himself
and his ranch in Uz
this.

I took from the bookmobile a King James edition,
which I told them I preferred.
Reading through it, it was as if I was there
in my own suffering and the reasons for it.
As if the stars over Uz was my own Uz.
Job's three friends,
and in the end, Elihu, a fourth,
that Job does not need as the three had more
than their say with Job wishing politely
they would leave.

On his hacienda with servants tending what was left—
who would plow the fields and plant the crops—
and open the creek after stones rolled over and piled up
and would flood a field in the next storm.

If only it was as it had been with Job secure
until Satan came in the form of whirlwind, fire,
Chaldeans in three bands, and Sabeans,
floating in his helicopter in the clouds above Uz
to observe or poke the more obstinate camels
from the enclosure of the large field
through broken fences
which the servants would repair after lifting all day
the stones out of the tributary to open the flow of the creek.

FUZZ

How hard to get up when you're wounded
not knowing if you can walk from the room—

but someone there. Someone missing.
Not a forest near. You sit in a chair to watch the ruffle

of sunlight through a tree at the window on its long
journey also. How single it stands— walking as if this

is the day the woodcutter divides the trunk from its
branches. A remnant on the table. A crumb the hornet might

buzz.

NOW YOU ARE MORE YOURSELF

You open the book
to three friends, Eliphaz, Bildad, Zophar, talking
on the portico of the hacienda. A few flamingos in the yard.

Servants raking leaves
with the soothing sound of a rake sweeping gravel
or scraping boils
if Job could reach
the elevating pain
the humiliation in front of friends
who nick him with their words.

Could he talk to someone else?—
his wife hiding in the kitchen
or making herself scarce in her room.

What could she say to alleviate?

She was in over her ears and cried to herself in her room
between the large wardrobe and the wall
she could wedge herself between—
if he opened the door he could not see her—
if she could stop her weeping and be quiet.

TOUCHING THE ALMIGHTY, WE CANNOT FIND HIM OUT— JOB 37:23

I go forward, but he is not there; and backward, but I cannot perceive him: On the left hand, where he works, but I cannot behold him; he hides himself on the right hand, that I cannot see him— JOB 23:8–9

It was now
the three friends
would not

give up.
Boils hurt.
Shoulder sore.

Library work undone.
Let them
not wake

from time
or go without their
questions.

EXTIRPATE

Touch all that he hath— JOB 1:11

It was near Bismarck.
A cherry-red fort from which soldiers rode.
A long line of cavalry.
The officers reading the field guide.
This way to the Indians.

After a binocularly look across the plains.
Another few days' ride.
How far until they were there?

He thought it would be all right.
But what in the distance?— Job and a story of trial.
They were not interested in Scripture.
Their wool uniforms cozy enough
began to itch in the mid-day heat.

Not enough for them to waste on riding.
As they tried to reach their goal of extermination.
The hills were tremendous to cross.
The horses needed rest.
To be ridden constantly from the fort across the fields.
Rust already in the trees.
Twirling before their eyes.

The cartwheel of navy blue, forest green, and black.
And what summation provided?
It was locked in the trees— those keepers of history.
The black hills behind them. The cherry fort.
The navy blue uniforms on the ridge
above the encampment of their destination.

VERSIONS OF THE MANY-VERSIONS-OF-GREASY-GRASS

1. SWIMMERS

. . . he that swimmeth spreadeth forth his hands to swim—
ISAIAH 25:11

We circled all around them swirling like water around a stone—
TWO MOONS, NORTHERN CHEYENNE

There is more than one story of the Battle at Little Bighorn. There are stories of the birds. The gophers and moles. There are stories of two women pushing their sewing awls into the ears of Custer when he was dead. Thou liftest me up to the wind; thou causest me to ride upon it, and dissolvest my substance—JOB 30:22. There are stories not knowing which soldier Custer was. He wore buckskin and had cut his hair. How could they know with so many? Some soldiers drowned in the Little Bighorn trying to cross the river with its high bank. Nothing certain in battle but differing U.S. Army reports. The Indian tribes had gathered for safety in numbers— Lakota, Arapaho, Hunkpapa, Santee, Oglala, Brulé, Minniconjou, Blackfeet, Northern and Southern Cheyenne— against five companies of the 7th Cavalry. The tribes were not going to return to the reservation— angered over settlers' intrusion on their land. But Custer was determined on his round-up until he realized he was outnumbered. The Indians seemed to grow from the ground as grass. Stories begat stories, transforming the battle into breaking parts. The earth was a place everyone wanted, though there was land as far as anyone could see. Enough for the paltry men on the battlefield running / shouting. The air full of smoke from guns and dust from horses' feet. What strange mating dance was this? What battle for territory? The animals took cover in the storm of a different kind. Rattlesnake. Elk. Pronghorn antelope. The sharp-tailed grouse with its brown and white spirit patterns like spots of snow across the hills in winter. The cottontail with other burrowers. All of them said, *Let them have the war to themselves.* It was women digging turnips who saw the soldiers coming— the way dust storms rise in wind or clouds battle with themselves leaving hailstones and the fierce needles of rain. A late Sunday afternoon— July 25, 1876— maybe 7,000 Indians and Brevet Major General George Custer with his captains, lieutenants, horse soldiers, surgeons, his Crow and Arikara scouts at the Battle of the Little Bighorn the Indians called *Greasy Grass.* Some of the Indians had been swimming when Custer inserted the cavalry where it didn't belong, the way Israeli artist Sigalit Landau made a closet of the Dead Sea, submerging a black, high-neck, ankle-length dress into the sea for two months, allowing it to crystallize, changing what could have been a funeral dress into a wedding dress. Custer died on the backbone of the hill. His own dear bride, Libbie, at Fort Abraham Lincoln several hundred miles away. Or Custer died in the river where Buffalo Calf Trail Road Woman knocked him from his horse. Even Indians don't agree when history split into as many versions as there were Indian tribes. Custer died with bullets in his head and chest. No one knows why he was not mutilated or scalped. None of the Indians were sure which body was Custer's but they knew he was there. Little Killer remembered the warriors sang—

Long Hair, Long Hair,
we were short of guns, and you brought us many.

11

The past is a natatorium. To sort through history is to move through water. To look at the Little Bighorn is difficult as taking off a wet swimsuit and putting dry clothes on a damp body.

2. THE REVISIONISTS

> *Hurrah boys, we've got them!*
> *We'll finish them up and then go home to our station—*
> GENERAL GEORGE CUSTER

What took place was a series of tactical errors.
The conclusion of two days of battle was 263 troopers dead.
Over the past decades an intertwining of Indian history has occurred.
White Cow Bull claimed to have shot him.
Big Nose said he killed him.
No, the wife of Spotted Horn Bull spoke.
Runs-Him, Goes-Ahead, Hairy-Moccasin had their versions
of Custer riding down the Medicine Tail Coulee
and then toward the river where he probably planned to ford.
Now the Indians had discovered him.
Custer was forced to turn and head for the hill
where he would make his famous last stand.
No, Pretty Shield, wife of Goes-Ahead, said Custer died in the water
of the Little Bighorn with Two-Bodies and the blue soldier
carrying his flag.
It is truth that lies scattered for this new world.

3. CHIEF GULL RECOUNTS GREASY GRASS ON THE HILL WHERE IT HAPPENED

If I could have one dance
it would be that one
enough to hold me through the winters that followed.

It was the dark ages after that.
Buffalo gone. Our will to thrive.
We never won another battle.

The winds that followed blew us into little cut-out houses.
Fold-back doors. Little plastic buffalo.
Cowboys still after.

4. 7TH CAVALRY HORSE CEMETERY

> *On top of Custer Hill was a circle of dead horses. Around Custer
> some 30 or 40 men had fallen, some of whom had used their horses as
> breastworks—*
> LT. EDWARD S. GODFREY, COMPANY K, 7TH CAVALRY,
> ARRIVING TWO DAYS AFTER THE BATTLE, JULY 27, 1876
>
> *I had all the horse bones gathered and placed in a mound—*
> CAPT. G.K. SANDERSON, 11TH INFANTRY, APRIL 7, 1879

It was 14 miles from the ridge where Custer saw the Indian encampment
to the valley of the Little Bighorn. He didn't know the hills and gullies

that lay between. We were out of breath when we came over the last hill and saw the large encampment. More horses with them than with us. When the battle raged the soldiers shot us for barriers to hide behind. They were far outnumbered. There was nothing else to do. They knew they would not survive to ride away. The wind came up the hill from the cottonwoods of the Little Bighorn— *Shuuu. Shuuu.* Now you can catch your breath.

ALTERNATIVE FACTS

The friends sat seven days with Job—
[the former owner of sheep and camels
now desolate also of children].
Bildad reviewed his notes
with friends.
Chomping at the dialogue.
They preferred monologue.
If we can speak to you [how could we
hold back?— JOB 4:2]—
There was a lot of talking then.
You have strengthened many.
Now you fold when you're
in trouble?
You can't be innocent, Job.
Zophar and Eliphaz agree.
Their different thoughts
blaming Job
in what could be called an unfair debate.

HISTORY (2) BY INTERLOCUTORY

for John James' "History (n.)"

He didn't want to come to writing, but the blank page enticed him. He could cover it with pencil-lead. The yellow flick of pencil. It always was the hornet nest of history. [He] *often need*[ed] *something to write against in order to write at all. Strictures* [were] *good for* [him]. [He] *grabbed a few books* [he] *knew to be relevant to the ideas on which* [he] *was meditating—tomes by Hegel, Haruki Murakami, Anne Carson, and others—and started excerpting text that for various reasons seemed to interest* [him], *using it to fill out the prose block when* [he] *got stumped. That's what the italicization was about. It's all excerpted text.* [He] *composed on* [his] *computer, as a single prose block consisting of 16 lines in Perpetua font.* History after all is from histurry, meaning stirred together with legerity. History is a long tale. A scattered record of events. Often explaining the need for excerption.

MAY IT WORK.

May it. May it— Custer said as he charged Custer Hill.
He would have named his daughter Mayit.

MY OWN UZ

La condition humaine, *1933*
René Magritte [Belgian]1898–1967
National Gallery of Art, Washington

A path continues from the easel to the outdoor scene.
A *trompe l'œil*.
Job's friends painted their path on his.

A sock always slipping down the heel
into the shoe.
Or his view into theirs

when God's voice as a bird flew through
the window
from the painting on the easel.

SOMETIMES A DOOR CLOSES IN ITS PLACE.

Even before the wall is built. The windows open. A breeze learns how to blow. It is concerned with moving curtains. With pushing papers on the floor. Turning up a corner of the tablecloth. All of it. Not even out of breath.

Acorns fall on the roof before it is shingled. She heard the clatter. The shutters were in place though not the walls. Boards shiplap the ceiling. In the street a loppy catalpa drops its large leaves. They could be supper plates for the table.

Dearest General beloved one— I write U this letter of the highest flame even as the hills are burning.

PART TWO

ABSTRACT

The essay is an avant-garde study of the Old Testament Book of Job— using the practice of poetics to get to meanings that float under the surface of written language— or maybe above. A meta-poetry.[2] An unorthodox meeting of roads. Job and the Native American experience of loss. Poetics and its undertow. A sometimes incomplete structure that leaves meaning open to allow other meanings that would otherwise be ignored. A sufficiency of gap-work.

Suffering changes boundaries. I sought an unconventional form in which to write that would message the text. Form in tandem with con-text— not just a container for it— but a fluid and fragmentary act on its own. As Job muttering in his suffering as he struggled to understand God's purpose.

I am after a fundamental language haunted by its subtext.

---

[2] Actually, narrative poetry is the meta-poetry. Its meaning usually is clear— and outside the more abstract and obtuse poetry, with meanings between and within other meanings, which is where poetry should be.

MORE THAN CONTENT IS THE MANNER IN WHICH IT IS HELD

In the Sky
I am walking,
A Bird
I accompany.

"A Chippewa Dream Song" recorded by Frances Densmore, American
Indian Prose and Poetry, *edited by Margot Astrov, Capricorn Books,
New York, 1962, originally published as* The Winged Serpent, *1946.*

I am writing about writing about Job and the Book of Job which has
haunted me— the poetics of it that takes the praxis of poetics to think
in another way— to write about— and still not thoroughly.

Somehow it is tied up also in the Native American experience—
haunted by the past.

Haunted, from the 1200–50 Middle English *haunten.*
Old French *hanter,* to frequent.
Old Norse *heimta,* to lead home.

A doublant of meaning which poetry explores— frequently haunting
the road that leads to a house in the woods under the coverage of trees
lapping over one another in critical overlaps at times. A creative bri-
colage of words pointing in various directions to the junction. Itself
sending others to various outward places. A plane station. Or airport.

As Job is in one place, Uz, that has been traveled to and upon and from within and without as a transport of given text from an origin in oral tradition to multiple authorships over the years to the written state in which it now abides in the Old Testament of the Bible.

A pivotal book— why men suffer has been asked since the beginning. Right there with *Let there be light*— is followed by the suffering of that incoming light. And here we stand at the junction.

Job's lamentations are similar to Native American lamentations, a literature I taught for years. Wherefore is light given to him that is in misery, and life unto the bitter in soul; Which long for death, but it comes not— JOB 3:20–21.

A wolf
I considered myself,
But the owls are hooting
And the night
I fear.
[Collected by Frances Densmore from the Chippewa, *American Indian Prose and Poetry*]

A warrior
I have been.
Now
It is all over.
A hard time
I have.
[Sitting Bull's last song upon surrendering to the United States authorities after the Custer Massacre, *American Indian Prose and Poetry*]

Both lamentations have the frequency of home. Of hitting home. Of the frequency of haunting, which is something that returns again and again to which is the meaning of. The sojourn of it back to. To lead to the place of. To the loner on earth. Man shut up in his own and different circumstances.

A crossing of the study of the Old Testament Book of Job that washes into the New Testament. I claim here Christ as going back to Job— though he was before that book also— from the beginning he was. I know my redeemer lives, and that he shall stand at the later day upon the earth— JOB 19:25. The foretelling of the junction between God and men on earth. A bombastment of the gospel of good news that cannot be fathomed by anyone who has never heard of Christ. Or minimally heard. Or who has been scorched in boarding school. The bones of children still are being recovered at Carlisle Industrial Indian School in Pennsylvania, and returned to families. Or unknown bones meaning unknown to whom they belonged and returned to unknown graves.

It is said that many children on the train from North Dakota to Carlisle Indian Industrial School sang their death song. After the loss of buffalo, their land, and way of life. Followed by separation from family.

Job is an Old Testament Indian disposed of 7,000 sheep. 3,000 camels. 500 yoke of oxen. 500 asses. 10 children. All of that lost to be educated in God's school of this-is-the-way-it-is. It is for your own good, mission-aries, teachers, evangelists, and zealots said.

Poetry is cartography. An imagined mapping of the wilderness for an understanding of the wilderness, or as much of the wilderness as can be understood. As if Christianity was closer to understanding, and not full of nettles itself— as the many denominations and interpretations of the Christian texts testify. Maybe Christianity is more accessible than poetry, especially the abstract poetry that sometimes defies understanding. As if Christianity didn't defy understanding, also.

But God says that his thoughts are not our thoughts, neither are his ways our ways— ISAIAH 55:8. We are made in his image— but there is crawl space between the image and the real— as God sent his son to a beleaguered people God had created in the first place with a full blast of the I-will intact. But the loving God killed his son and placed judgment on him and then resurrected him and us with him— if we believe on his name. What is difficult about that?

Poetics has these particles within it. An eruption of a momental understanding in language.

We were made in the image of God, and as small particles of God we could think for ourselves. The self-will is acted upon and indeed we are the image of the free-willed free-thinker, but without the stuff of holiness knocked out of us by our decision to follow our own way. But all is not lost after 4,000 years of prophets bellowing their warnings of doom. Eventually Jesus came to the earth to clarify. He was a replica of God. To believe in him was to believe in the God we could not see, and thereby we are saved from the everlasting damnation we have found ourselves in. Or have found in ourselves.

Of course, the Bible is translation for original languages, and also caught in different translations of those original languages, and has lost a lot of what there is to lose. But a kernel is there to be looked at.

Native children were given Biblical names in boarding schools. Luther Standing Bear, for instance. Maybe it was reverse appropriation. Christian appropriation. The boys were now Matthew. Mark. Luke. John. Ezekiel. Zephaniah. Haggai.

When tribal roles were taken, Native names often were shortened. Bird-with-yellow-streak-down-its-tail was written Yellowtail. An erasure of identity. The bird-with-yellow-streak-down-its-tail captured a phenomenon. As the bird changed into flight, there was a flash of yellow feathers. The name had momentum. A structure of going-into-motion. It was what was taken away with the name change. Other subtleties of verbiage integral to a sense of purpose were lost. Exploration of those rifts, in part, is what poetics has as its destination. It also was the purpose of Job's suffering— in that he would travel the rift between man's understanding of suffering (i.e., Job had sinned) and God's purpose in Job's suffering (i.e. that Job might see more clearly his place in God's being).

But the purpose of these changes for the Indian was to facilitate the turn of Native into Christian. Into literate.

The unevenness of it. In the early days it was not abundant.

Intent was there, but the cruelty of boarding schools and indoctrinations left their marks upon the generations. Left their shifts of thought, which is what abstract poetics is full of anyway. Poetics as the dis-arrangement of words until the standard text is torn as the renting of a robe— JOB 1:20.

I wonder how often Job remembered his months of trial in the years of restoration that followed. The suffering. God must love suffering because he sent Job suffering, and his own son suffered— and the son then said he would show the Apostle Paul what he must suffer— ACTS 9:16. And how God himself must suffer over us whom he created with choice in our heads.

There is an outpost of poetics in the Bible, too—
I see men as trees, walking— MARK 8:24—
is similar to the awkward structure of the wind only I am afraid of.
[Frances Densmore, from the Chippewa recordings]

Sometimes
I go about pitying myself
While I am carried by the wind
Across the sky.
Again—
[Densmore, from the Chippewa recordings]

There is an immense loneliness in these passages. Had tornadoes swept the prairie? The Cavalry? Had the *I* been afraid of being swept away also?— as maybe tepee, buffalo, horse had been.

The separation of thought from the summations around it— the cream separated from the milk. When I was a child, milk was delivered to the door. A *thickness* was in the neck of the glass bottle. The clotted cream had to be poured out first.

The *I* that pities itself becomes one with the swirling winds beneath the sky. Is this a literal taking? Imaginative? Figurative? He may be without his tribe, but maybe he is closer to the place where the powers dwell.

I remember another piece in which the *I* heard the trees singing as though they were men. In JOB 38:7, it is the morning stars that sing. That nature has a voice— that all beings have voice is known. Did not the donkey speak to Balaam in NUMBERS 22:28–30?

It is the biblical passage, I see men as trees, walking— as seeing something, but not yet fully knowing what was seen. We are in the process of the journey. The act of migration is the praxis of poetry. We learn to see. We learn we can see. We learn what to see.

It is the poetics of experience that is speaking at the root of poetry and its practice. Getting at the truth that seems to be moving as we get close to seeing it.

That is the energy-field in poetics. The writing of it. The reading. The haunting experience of poetics.

The *I* is a blind man because we are blind. We cannot see things as they are. We are in the shadows. Darkly— I CORINTHIANS 13:12.

It was in Mark 8:24 that Jesus put spittle on the blind man's eyes. Then Jesus put his hands on the man again, who afterwards saw men walking as men walk— reaching that spit of land in the sea of the blindness of man.

Poetics separates the bone from the marrow— HEBREWS 4:12. It separates the words of a sentence. It makes known the things between. It works something like the subconscious works in our conscious lives. Something to the side of. The haunting of which haunts. The home of it. The particular poetics of the lamentations of Job in Uz and the Native American on the North American continent are my heritage. A personal sense of loss. A preponderance for suffering that lasts in the whole world. A trip to Syria several years ago. The Middle East. Eastern Europe. Pine Ridge. I-70 across Ohio in a snowstorm that was at times perilous, though nothing compared to the civil war in Syria. Other travels to places that have known hardship— usually solitary travels to sites of historical massacres. The voice of the land also remembers. [And the land rested from war— JOSHUA 11:23— as though it took part in the battle.] An inclination to think upon these issues. To fit poetics into these narrow margins and bifurcations and marginal dips along the way. And yet a faith that overcomes all. It is beyond reason. It is what poetics is. And the practice of it that is a substantiation that makes its subjects in its own way. Poetics and the practice of it as a small insignia of the great work of the cross. Something that purveys. That stays over a lifetime.

The *I* in Job can be seen in part as Indian. A tribal man separated from his tribe during trial— layered into layers in a redundancy of suffering to relocate the self in relationship to the self of God. A rite ordained by God in Christ.

As Job found his own vacancy, after the loss of children, herds, his place at the gate of the city of Uz. A benefactor who suddenly found his hacienda empty except for a few servants here and there trying to stay out of sight, trying not to notice Job in his pitiful state covered with boils and ashes and dust.

Did they even recognize him? His three friends— Eliphaz, Bildad, and Zophar—did not upon their arrival— JOB 2:12. Yet they sat down with him upon the ground for seven days and seven nights, and none spoke to him for they saw his grief.

By 1880, some 30 to 60 million buffalo were killed so train tracks could cross the prairie, and wagon trains unimpeded, and early cattle ranchers could fence their land and farmers could break the sod and plant crops. The boarding schools that stripped Native language and culture left the children vacant inside. Unable to nourish their children when they had them. Bereft of the language that held together the multi-fibers of existence.

The Native prairie and the likeness of Job's compound in Uz.

He walked the barren fields, pastures, paddocks, barns, sheds. Kicked a knot or clump of bunch grass, fescue, bindle, bent grass, wheat grass, blue grass. He missed meetings of the Uz city council. He cleaned out his deceased children's houses. Found one of his daughter's dolls saved in a trunk for her own daughter that would never come. Job smoothed the grass clumps left in a shadow of the sun. The waiting criticism of the friends when they started into Job, leaving wisdom on the train.

Acceptance to God's kingdom is built on substantiation— the substitute of Christ for the real crucifixion of man as the people who knew not they were God's people.

Job as Job and Job as symbol of struggle before a Godhead which cannot be undone, but through which can be learned the chasm and therefore align the salient one to his true place in the universe.

On a trans-Jobian plane— the subsequent instruction of God to Job to pray for his three friends, Eliphaz, Bildad, and Zophar— JOB 42:8–9. They had to bring seven bulls and seven rams to Job for a burnt offering. Job had now attained a likeness to the intercessor. He prayed for the friends. As he also had covered his children with prayer— JOB 1:5— that for a while worked until the whirlwind got in the way, taking his blessed assurance.

Job's prayer for his children was not effectual in saving his children. Yet Job is an intercessor in whom we learn our distance from the Godhead. To realize our distance from God is to recognize the first step in reconciliation. I am here. You are there. An intercessor must be present for us to meet. But now in Christ Jesus ye who once were far off are made nigh by the blood of Christ— EPHESIANS 2:13

After the intolerable attitude in the noble Job was exposed— Now they that are younger than I hold me in derision, whose fathers I would have disdained to have set with the dogs of my flock— JOB 30:1. For want and famine they were solitary, fleeing into the wilderness in former time desolate and waste— JOB 30:3. Here again, the tie to the Native American fleeing the Cavalry. It is easy to see through the poetic imagination the homeless in Uz and the Indian on the Great Plains of America seeking shelter and hiding places in ravines, embankments, and caves along hillsides.

In Job, I write the memory of an event at which I was not present. I write a group of incongruities. By using contemporary terms— a hacienda in Uz on Coots Ranch Road I saw once driving in Texas and thought to bring the present into the past. As the past often pokes its way into the present.

More than content is the manner in which it is held.

Early Native poetry/song came as abstraction— as parts separated from the whole. As dreams which were often considered more reliable than what could be seen. A man had to dream before he could act. Then he had to act out in ceremony what he had dreamed, before the actual act that he performed in battle or whatever the dream called for. It is the poetics of Job. Which resulted in turning from blindness to knowledge. Which often takes discomfort to dislodge.

It is the extracted— the dissociated— that is the fabric of poetics. Though poetry has many forms. Some of it narrative. But the abstract poems are closest to the Native origin of poetics. The visions from another place trying to reach.

A dislocation of the self into the folds of the Godhead. A whirlwind beyond understanding.

Shall mortal man be more just than God? Shall a man be more pure than his maker?— Eliphaz asks in JOB 4:17.

Yet there is an arrogance in man, and a confidence of his own power, that has to be reckoned with.

I am walking the wind.
With a long stick
We are walking.

Yes, even I can move the universe. I can do all things through Christ which strengthens me— PHILIPPIANS 4:13. Again the puzzling dichotomy of Christian faith.

Such was the behavior of the Christian invaders onto the prairie with their wagon-trains and muskets. They gave the Indian land-treaties. Making paper of land. Making land of absence. It is part of America's history. Yet— can you imagine America remaining in its wilderness while the rest of the world marched on? It was going to happen— what happened. Often forgotten in history lessons— but by the Indian— who cries out at times as Job did in his trials.

Often the Indian signed without being able to read the words, but believing what they were told. America is land stolen for the glory of God. The Old Testament God of their-land-is-your-land. Go take it. I am with you. It is hard to swallow. It is what haunts. It is what home means. Living with the unsatisfied. The incompleted understanding.

Poetics leaves the unsaid on the page. Especially Native poetry, which is the mere outline of thought. Of the form addressed. It is its holy aspect.

He stretches out the north over the empty place, and hangs the earth upon nothing. He binds up the waters in his thick clouds, and the cloud is not rent under them— JOB 26:7–8.

Look when nothing to see. Even emptiness is alive with spirit. A great raking. To see the branches bared of leaves. Or to see the leaves without their branches. To see the structure without its leaves is what poetics is.

A practice of transition of loss and assimilation into something of what it is not. The words remade. Retooled. Revisited.

And your ears shall hear a word behind you saying, This is the way, walk you in it when you turn to the right hand, or when you turn to the left— ISAIAH 30:21.

A word will speak? I thought it was something to be spoken by another. These are parts of his ways— JOB 26:14.

He claps his hands among us— JOB 34:37. A whirlwind that is itself a whirlwind writing about a whirlwind in a whirlwind.

Eventually Elihu, the fourth of Job's friends, shows up— Elihu the Buzite to Job the Uzite— There is a spirit in man: and the inspiration of the Almighty gives them understanding— JOB 32:8. Yes, there is something in us that is a landing field for the Almighty. Often it has to be plowed.

Job spends all of chapter 29 recounting his exploits— When I went out to the gate through the city, when I prepared my seat in the street! The young men saw me, and hid themselves: and the aged arose and stood up. The princes refrained talking, and laid their hand on their mouth. The nobles held their peace, and their tongue cleaved to the roof of their mouth— JOB 29:7–10. Job continues with his exploits— then God in chapters 38–41 recounts his exploits— Where were you when I laid the foundations of the earth?— JOB 38:4.

Wherefore I abhor myself and repent in dust and ashes, he concludes.— JOB 42:6

I am ashamed before the earth;
I am ashamed before the heavens;

I am ashamed before the dawn;
I am ashamed before the evening twilight;
I am ashamed before the blue sky;
I am ashamed before the sun;
I am ashamed before *that standing within me which speaks with me.*

Old Torlino, a Navajo priest, from the Introduction, *American Indian Prose and Poetry*, in which the editor, Margot Astrov, says that Indian texts translated from Native language cannot actually be translated because of the difference in thought structure. She also quotes Ruth Underhill [anthropologist, 1883–1984]—

A translation of language "so different from ours in all its devices as is an Indian tongue has much to answer for. The entire way of thought is different. So are the grammatical forms and the order of words. One can hope to make the translation exact only in spirit, not in letter . . ."

It is the spirit of poetics that clangs against an unorthodox method of writing. What is more unorthodox than thought?

PART
THREE

I was not in safety, neither had I rest,
neither was I quiet, yet trouble came— JOB 3:26

I HAVE SEWED SACKCLOTH TO
MY SKIN– JOB 16:15

A man comes to a new
chapter unlike
the old.

Not chapter
but characters—
Eliphaz, Bildad, Zophar, the three friends
Elihu, a fourth
Job's wife
the daughters

Job— I am innocent— JOB 33:9
Elihu— Job has spoken without knowledge—
My desire is that Job may be tried to the end— JOB 34:35–36

I WILL DROP BY UNANNOUNCED

They are at their willful dialogue
they all talk too loud
and had burritos
for supper at the table
their tiredness overbearing.

It was her house too.

Their innocence still a field away.

SHE WAS FIRST TO SPEAK

Job talks with his friends.
Would they ask me to join them?
I stand silent as a wind turbine on the high plains.
Where are my words that lift the flat sheet of the world
to address the suffering and dilemmas?
They leave me out.
To be without words!
The stubbles hurt my feet.
The Universe ate our first children.[3]
We all are expendable.
This Mystery. This Unanswerable.
This Old One up there who spoke the world into being.
But I remain silent?
What skies are these? To whom do they belong?
Tell me where you are. What you see.
What God is there with Satan rolling around his throne saying, give
me Job for a moment?[4]
Are there other worlds? Isn't this one enough?
All those buzzings of comets and falling stars in the observatory in Uz.
Those astro-heads. Those Job's friends.
I would join the arguments if I had their bag of words.

[3] JOB 1:18–19
[4] JOB 1:11, 2:3–4

BUTTER BEANS

We didn't know the storm was upon us.
We thought it was the rattle of cattle trucks
from Coots Ranch Road.
We didn't know the wind stirred clouds over the hacienda in Uz.
But the storm blew over the house, hop-jawed and whip-jacked
in its steel-toed boots.
It blew out windows. Collapsed the roof.
We knew too late.
God had come with his beam-splitter plugged in.
He bent light waves. He melted metal.
He lifted us above the sky over the Coots Ranch Road
far from the land of Uz.
What protest or accusation could we make?
What does Job see now through the parchment
he tubes for his telescope?
Does he look for us?
What does he hear those nights under the stars?
The Bear— Arcturus— the Bootes where our father looks?
Over us, the Big One strums his noise all night
Our father listens—
an upright man who suffered loss.
We were his first daughters, happy as butter beans.
Now we watch God's headlights on the road at night.
We know the line of snow against the bottom of the window.
The string-line stars.
The memory of us hangs like icicles from the gutters in Uz.

The friends, Eliphaz,[5] Bildad,[6] Zophar,[7] will hit our father
when he is down—
talking of the relativity of simultaneity,
footnoting him to death.
Job worships the God he speaks to, a guitar on his knee—
What do we hear in the Universe but microbes buzzing?
Does Job remember his daughters playing—
how it was to watch the path of matted grass
as we ran through the field?

[5] JOB 4:1
[6] JOB 8:1
[7] JOB 11:1

JOB, THE COMET MAN

Ground Control to Major Tom— DAVID BOWIE

The stars shuffed off their light like snakeskin.
I sit in darkness. Oh that my words were engraved
with an iron pen and lead in the rock forever[8]
and my struggle to get beyond Arcturus was known—
that kite constellation with a lightning rod at its corner.

He garnished the heavens, yet formed the crooked snake.[9]
Who can understand? I lost everything I had.
I am mocked by boys. I am accused of suffering
because of wrongdoing. But God does what He does.
He tries whom He tries.

There is a path no fowl knows which the falcon's eye
has not seen.[10] The heavens are full of falcon's eyes.
My wife thinks they are the eyes of her first children,
but they are stars in this traveling corral where we are
kept until God calls.

There is Big-Time life beyond the battlefield of this Earth.
I know it in the flow tube that the brain is.

[8] JOB 19:24
[9] JOB 26:13
[10] JOB 28:7

These b-fields of rotary motion— The Unmovable One
with a b-bomb up His sleeve moving against J-prime— me.

I sit on this ash heap. I scrape my boils, these b-blisters,
these robes of fright. What craziness, these ideas—
God is one straight line through another. He rolls the truth
of His axioms. He speaks in voices from His zone.

What b-swarm do I see in my telescope? What eyeball
with a voice??— I recalculate the change in velocity
through this darkness— I get it then. B-balmed. B-fit.
I hear His strings singing the Universe not once out of beat.

STORIATION

They are standing on the bridge though there is no river. They feel however they have been swimming. They are without children now. They are shadows of themselves. Their shadows disconnect from their bodies. They watch their shadows blowing here and there. Sometimes the storm lifts its head in the uprising of dust from the river-bed. What do they know of tornado warnings interrupting newscasts? Or the story of Noah in Spanish on a late-night channel when there is no sleep? Actually, the flood is mentioned in the Book of Job.[11] Wherever Uz was no one is sure.[12] The time not clear either. Maybe among the oldest in the Bible.[13] Wherever it was, it was the beginning of inquiry— the reason for suffering. They had been through a calamity. A disaster, actually. It was hard to recover. They were not doing a good job. Withdrawing from one another, which is typical. Who wants to be with someone in a mess they only want distance from? Where is *paper* to write sorrow and loss to make a story of— a storiation of? Who writes the report after all— the act of suffering to document the tract? How many drafts until a shadow floats clean of its body?

---

[11] JOB 12:15 He withholds the waters, and they dry up: also he sends them out, and they overturn the earth.
JOB 22:15–16 Have you marked the old way which wicked men have trodden? Which were cut down out of time, whose foundation was overflown with a flood.
JOB 27:20 Terrors take hold on him as waters.
JOB 28:4 The flood breaks out from the inhabitant; even the waters forgotten by the foot; they are dried up, they are gone away from men.
[12] Uz could have been in Saudi Arabia, Southern Syria, Southwestern Jordan, Southern Israel.
[13] Job could have been a grandson of Jacob. Genesis 46:13— And the sons of Issachar: Tola, and Puvah, and Job, and Shimron.

FRIENDS ARRIVE

It is not likely, they said,
to be in it for nothing.
The stars are far up.

How high they are— JOB 22:12.
He started the car.
Before him the uncertainty.

He endured the taunts.
Willing to let go.
Wherever relief was.

The words they say are steadfast breeze.
Not kingdoms of the world.
Nor stones. Nor bread.

ELIPHAZ, BILDAD, ZOPHAR

With clouds he covers the light, and commands it not to shine
by the cloud that comes between— JOB 36:32

It all had been seen before.
But they put the bullet points on the wall.
The bulletin along the bottom on the screen
to add to the usual programming.
A passage with possible incident.
A disruption in scheduling to make it more
than what it really was.

They were standing before Job himself.
Deliverers of news which they forswore
they never wanted to deliver.

Behold the cloud higher than thou— JOB 35:5.
Who can understand the spreading— JOB 36:29.

ELIHU THE WEATHER-MAN ARRIVES

He is interested in weather—
Snow— JOB 37:6
Rain— JOB 37:6
Whirlwind— JOB 37:9
Cold— JOB 37:9
Frost— JOB 37:10
South wind— JOB 37:17

Does he review the year's forecast?
Or give a year's weather at one time?

From his storm-chaser, Elihu reports a barn flying northward over a farmer's field.

He sends the people of Uz running for their basements that have disappeared in their dream and made assessments of their situation, which is dire for the storm cometh, and Elihu, who is not one of the group of Job's three friends, and younger than they, ordains them to listen as he seems to be forerunner of what is coming— the voice of the Lord God himself. Who would ask the complainant Job, Where werest thou when I laid the foundations of the earth?— JOB 38:4.

BEHEMOTH SPEAKS FOR HIMSELF
AND LEVIATHAN[14]

God sets Job straight. He lets him know that God
is God. And Job is plague in Hazmat suit.
Well, not exactly that. But Job is in
deep water. God says, Can you send the light-
ning? Can you clothe the horse with thunder? Now
let Behemoth a few words speak. The mar-
gin says that Behemoth is elephant.
His tail is cedar and the sinews of
his stones are wrapped together. Here I pause.
I must be something else than elephant
that has a scraggly tail. My force is in
my navel, and my bones are strong as i-
ron. I am chief among the ways of God.
The shade trees cover me with shadows. Wil-
lows of the brook surround me. I can drink
a river. I have more to say but God
is in a rush to reach the end of ar-
gument, make mildew of the insolence
as Job insists on innocence. But who
among them is the innocent? Not one—
the point God makes. If time was mine I would
have said that Job has had a cakewalk. God
continues much too soon, and asks if Job

[14] JOB 40:15– JOB 41:34

can pull Leviathan with hook? Or catch
his tongue on cords? Or make a covenant
with him? Or fill his skin with barbs? Or head
with spears? There's no one fierce enough to stir
him up. His scales are shut. No air can come
between. His flakes of flesh are joined. They can-
not move. Can this be whale? And why does he get
more time than Behemoth? Leviathan
upturns the deep. A path shines after him
as if the sea were full of snow. Can Job
do anything like that? If there was time,
I could have said much more about myself.
But the apostrophes are his— Job's life.
Job's wife. Job's daughters, sons. Job's place in Uz.
Job's herds of camels, oxen, sheep, and ass.
He should be quarantined. Or work for Uz-
Electric as a lineman. Night divis-
ion. Unit F. Suquamish Reserva-
tion. Headache to the union. God moves on
until Job knows that God is God. And Job
is Job beneath him on the scale of things.
I could have made more argument, if there
was time for swill to settle, camps to form.

CERTAIN DAYS GAVE HIM TROUBLE

Mornings were difficult. Evenings dragged. It was not over when darkness came. Then the dreams took shape. His children in the whirlwind. The asymmetry of his face. Past reconciliations with the tasks at hand. Wife. Caliper. Hoe. Hay fork. Harrow. His shed with work-tools. Tractor. The servants' quarters. Fields for all the herds.

JEHORAH[15]

The oxen were plowing, and the asses feeding beside them—
JOB 1:14

Someone is in the garden— no one I can see.
The fur on the dog's back rises. I hear it growl.
Images pass in a dream, but I am awake.
Broad trousers made of sheep skin— unsheared.
A bare chest.
I am afraid.
The spirit moves among the saffron, henna, hyacinth, hibiscus.
He is there— there! All the dogs bark wildly.
The spirit is gone.

In the night wind shakes the house.
I hear a noise louder than the wind.
Job jumps from the bed—
There is a flash of light
as if the sun leapt over the house without following the dawn.
I hide my eyes in the covers. What is it?
Fire— Job answers.
The sky is burning.
Flames are eating the earth! Then the fire is gone.

---

[15] A name the author has given to the unnamed wife of Job. It should be noted that she is interested in making summations and having a voice of her own.

The birds stop their screeching— the dogs their barking—
and we are left with silence.

I hoped the children were in their houses.
I hoped the servants watching our flocks and herds
kept them from running.
All is well. The Lord God is with us.
He is a God of uprising— yes. But his hands are upon us.
Let the wind rock the house. Let the fire eat the sky.

In the dawn, a large tree has fallen in the pasture beyond the barn.
The roots of the overturned tree look like fingers
trying to reach back into the earth.

I see other trees shucked of their leaves.
Grape vines blown down. The almond and olive trees.
The flags and rushes smothered in the wetlands.

In the early light, Job goes with the servants
to look at the tree that fell.
I bring a meal to the field but he does not eat.
Sometimes I take bites as I sit near the men.

Someone is coming from the distance.
Now others are coming, one after another.

The Sabeans took the ox and asses
and killed the field servants.
The Chaldeans took the camels.
The fire of God fell from heaven and burned up the sheep.

A great wind from the wilderness blew down our son's house
and killed our seven sons and three daughters.

AHHHHHHHHHHHHH—

I fall in a mat of leaves in horror.
Twigs scratch my face as I twist among them.
I see Job struck to the ground with the news.
He stands up and tears his cloak and falls down again
and worships God.

The children— all ten of them? Not one survived?
A servant tries to wipe the leaves from my face and matted hair.
I swat her away.

Job cuts off his hair in odd patches with a knife
I brought with the meal.

Is God still in the sky? Maybe he isn't awake yet.
Maybe the storm frightened him and he stepped to another place.

Curse God and die— I say.

It is harrowing. Harrowing.
Shave your head, Job. You look like a broken hedge.

Job sends the house servants to borrow oxen from the neighbors.
He tells me to wait at the hacienda.
When the oxen arrive
he goes with the carts to bring the children back.

I see them coming from the distance.
They arrive in the yard.
The servants carry the bodies to the tables.
Our sons. Jedrah. Joram. Jothnael. Abam. Abiham. Nobuel. Noban.
Our daughters. Habiah. Hajiah. Jobina.

We close their eyes and mouths. We wash their bodies.
I see the injuries. The bruises. The broken bones. I choke on my sobs.
We anoint the bodies with ointment.
We wrap them with myrrh in the linen.

Job has opened the family tomb in the escarpment
at the edge of our land.
I see he has shaved his head. I see how small it is.

A line of people come from town.
Some of Job's brothers and sisters.
The mourners and musicians.
We put a wreath around the necks of the borrowed oxen
that pull the carts.

Job speaks at the funeral. My hope he removed like a tree—[16]
Then everyone is gone.

For weeks I dream of the loss of our children and all we have.
Did the Sabeans and Chaldeans use the blowing dust as cover?
Did they use the fire from heaven to see the herds and flocks?
Did they use the confusion to take the animals?

[16] JOB 19:10

I am angry with the Sabeans who killed the servants
and stole the oxen and asses.
The Chaldeans who killed the servants and took the camels.
I am angry with the wind.
I am angry with the fire.
I am angry with Job's brothers and sisters who left.
I am angry with Job.
I am angry with God.

*

Someone walks in the garden.
The dog's growl sounds like a chair leg scraping the floor.
The spirit does not know where to run but makes haphazard movements
through the rows, trampling what is left of the flowers.
I feel a chill. Then he is gone.

Job is struck with boils. He scrapes them with a potsherd.
The boils are on his feet. The top of his head.
They cover his body.
He cannot sit. He cannot stand. He cannot lie down.
His breath is noxious. The pus continues.
I barely can look at him.
How pitiful the pleading of his eyes toward the distant sky.

I hold to the servant girl as we walk around the compound.
The field and pastures in ruin.
Only the barns, the outer buildings, the house
and servant quarters remain.
We cross the path where the sheep walked

from the pens to the field.
We cross the road the camels traveled.
At least we have cows. Chickens.
And dogs with nothing but spirits to guard.

At night the pastures are dark.
Where are the campfires the field servants built
as they guarded the flocks and herds?
Where is the sky above them that once shined with stars?
Where are my children?
With God, Job says.

Job still is praising him. But he is stewing, too.

Soon they come— The friends.
I see the way they look at Job as if they don't know him.
Perhaps they don't. Job has changed.
But their look is curious,
as if they have to get close to see
every agonized line in his face before they know it is Job.
I watch from behind the curtain.
They sit with Job seven days without speaking.

Where are Job's brothers and sisters? Could they not visit?
Are we shunned by everyone but these three men?
They talk. They talk. They talk.
Naked I was. Naked I am.
Eliphaz, the Temanite. Bildad, the Shuite.
Zophar, the Naamathite. Job, the Uzite.

I am supposed to feed them.
To wipe the dust of their feet from the stones on the floor
of the house.

I push the chair across the floor. It makes a growling sound.
I pick up the chair, drop it, pound it on the floor in a fit of anger.
ERRRRRRRR!

I am riled. I am riled. This messiness. These jagged walls.
Even the squawking crows mock us.

There is no way to ignore it.
I heard the laughter at our son's house.
They all wanted to be together.
Their voices floated over the fields.
Jedrah invited his younger brothers and sisters to eat
and drink with him.
They were louder than the sheep, the camels and oxen.

Job prayed for our children each morning,
rising early to make an offering for any offense they committed.

I take flowers to their tomb.
Sometimes the dog barks.
The field dogs respond with their own barking.
The whole world is barking.
I bark until a servant hushes me.

*

What spirit is that laughing? The one with sheep-skin chaps.
The one who has no visible form. Only a flickering of light.

Eliphaz, Bildad, and Zophar stay in the quarters of the field servants
who were killed by the Sabeans and Chaldeans.

Job sleeps in another room. There is distance between us.
Our words do not like to be with one another.
I hardly breathe when we speak.
Where are the days Job came to me—
when I felt his hand open my night robe?

I hear Job in his room.
He dreams more wildly than me.

I have visions of fireballs falling from the sky.
My head cannot contain the fireballs in my thoughts.
If I look at the trees, I would set them on fire.

I wail for my three daughters and seven sons!
I slam the chair on the floor with fury. Let the jackals howl.
Where is God— the invisible one—
the one more invisible than the invisible me?

*

The spirit pokes a hole in the sky.
His toe through— foot through— leg through.
He is stuck. He kicks at the hole— hips through—
whoops— chaps caught on the rough edge.

He pries with his hands.
Now chest stuck.
Then he falls to the ground. PLOP.
He raises his fist to heaven—

The house servants are busy cooking for the men
as they talk in the courtyard of the compound.
Does Job think I know nothing of his pain?
I kick the chair on its side.
The servant girls cower in the corner of the kitchen.
Make the gruel thin— I tell them.
Leave out the spices. Use the hard bread.

Now a fourth man arrives to talk to Job— Elihu, the Buzite.
When will all their talk be done?

The women of Uz come to sit with me.
The women who still have their daughters and sons.
Or I sit in the courtyard doorway and listen to the men talk.
I pick at a spot on my robe.
How did it get there? In the cooking room? The garden?
Maybe a muddy print of the dog with its paw on my lap.

I feel tied to the chair.
My words are sorghum in my mouth.
The women bring me wool from their flocks to card
and wash and wind into a ball and put on the spindle and weave
thinking I need something to do.
The women I taught to weave.

Our hacienda sits on the plain of Uz.
It is low to the ground with a tile roof and trees.
Our barns and field lick the ground also.
The birds. Chickens. The dogs.

I hear Job say of his life— Swifter than a weaver's shuttle.
But he is not dead. He only wishes he was.
He cannot move without groaning.
He cannot walk without his stick.

The women weave, but I am not weaving with them.
My life moves slower than a goat with an udder full of milk.

Job will not give up.
I have thoughts also— thoughts I cannot say.
Most of all to women.
Or if I speak, I say something that I've already said.

*

The field dogs are barking. My own dog barks.
Is the spirit there?
Is God going to let the spirit kill Job?
What would my life be without him?
I could kill him if the spirit doesn't— to rid him of his suffering.

The clouds seem pinned to the sky.
Otherwise they would fall and smother us in our ruin.

What is it like to die?
Are we like sheep shivering after we are shorn?
But dying— that is different from death.

I curl up behind a chair. Even the servants cannot drag me out.
I am not here, God. Take your meanness someplace else.

What is faith when the mind is frozen?
I wish I could stay in my room
but I have to direct the servant girls from place to place
in the market.
I pull the scarf over my head when people point.
It is shame that burns like a boil.
I turn to the women who stare— I am Jehorah!
My husband, Job, is a leader in Uz—
remember what he has done for you.

I feel the pain of my words before they are spoken—
before they are given birth.
How can words carry what they have to convey?
They are camels under their burdens.

I am mostly silent now. Though I am seen by other women.
Not Job. Never him. Or this God I do not know.

Faith is a ball of wool full of dirt and briers before it is carded.
Send that to God.
I do not think he hears.

Mark it on parchment.
Roll it up and send it with the next caravan.

*

God is in the sorrow floating above us— or is it Satan?
It is hard to tell the spirits apart.
Maybe God does not let the spirit bother us now.
The dog no longer barks at the garden.

I stand at the door. I GROWL!
Should I tell God my viewpoint on unfairness?
We have differing opinions.

Now there is a whirlwind in the field.
The men turn away, covering their heads.
Dust hits the window. I close the back door.
It must be God. What else can he blow away?
But God clears his throat. There is the sound of it anyway.
Maybe God has been quiet so long he is hoarse.

Look at Eliphaz, Bildad, Zophar— wishing only
for a trout-stocked stream.

Then somehow they are gone.

*

Slowly, Job heals— but for the scars from his boils.
I see the shiny marks they left.

I touch them with my fingers. They feel slick.
Job's hair grows. His beard catches crumbs.
He is back inside the city gate.

Our flocks and herds somehow show up.
I hear the pounding of camel hooves on the road.
I don't know where they came from.
The sheep seem to trot back to Uz from the sky.
They fill the path from the field to their pens,
trampling the garden, the flowers, and the grape vines
I tied back up.
There are so many of them. Twice what we had!
Oxen thunder from the distance. The asses with them.

In the fields the crops rise from the ground.
Job no longer sleeps in another room.

I bear children again. Seven sons, the number we lost.
Then the girls— Jemima. Keziah. Keren-happuch.
My first daughters dead, gone to heaven,
come back, resurrected in beauty,
though I know it is not them.

Job's brothers and sisters visit.
I glare at them when they are not looking.

The camels bellow. The oxen are plowing.
The asses feeding beside them.

WITH DREAMS UPON MY BED

Illustration XI from Illustrations of the Book of Job, *William Blake* *[1825]*

He's on a bedroll like any cowboy on the range,
but here he's placed by a lake of fire.
God and the serpent hover over him.

It is God, the accuser, who points to the tablets
above the zigzagged lighting crawling through the sky.

Near Job's bedroll, the waves are tongues of flames
from which two demons reach up and hold onto Job
as if to pull him below.
The third demon simply lifts his chains to show him.

There are words written in the margins—
notes from the suffering Job— With Dreams upon my bed
thou scarest & affrightest me with Visions.[17]

Why do ye persecute me— and are not satisfied
with my flesh?[18]

God has a foot cloven as the cattle, or worse—

[17] JOB 7:14
[18] JOB 19:22

as if he's part devil himself.
Maybe it's not God but Satan himself transformed
into an Angel of Light & his Ministers into Ministers
of Righteousness!

No, that can't be right.
The shining one *is* God under whom Job lies flat
on his bedroll with the end curled up for a pillow—

My bones are pierced in me in the night season and my sinews
take no rest.[19]
Job is sandwiched between God and the flames.
Job is seeing what Job is made of.

But this serpent who opposeth and exalteth himself
above all that is called God or is Worshipped—
rests his head on God's arm.
This idea that God allows Satan to afflict us
is one that takes getting used to.

But it's God's arm that separates Job and the serpent.
Not all is lost, but still— what terror—
what blaze of terrible thoughts—
1) God wearing a serpent as if a fox-tail stole.
2) God letting Satan tempt Job taking all but his life.

What a mixed message to sort out—
What effort to understand the purpose of hoof and snake,
stone tablets and lightning.

[19] JOB 30:17

How can anyone get near the sheltering dangerous God
and trust in his benevolence?
What odd message is in this illustration in black and white?

Yet look— Job holds the hoof-pick of his words—
though worms destroy this body, yet in my flesh shall I see God.[20]
If ever a cattle drover had a song.

---

[20] JOB 19:26

COMET-MAN'S WIFE

What do I know of the God Job heard? What do I know of the universe?
I wait on the tarmac in Uz for my flight. What longing to be elsewhere
than this Earth— Why can't we just have Earth? But the terrible stars
thwock over us with their noise. They are bright and sharp as bee-stings.
I swat them. What bee-blaze before us? What sting, this Earth? I watch
Job suffer. I have no investment in this. He saw something I did not—
We hold these multiple views of the Universe. He talks to God but I see
no one there. His convulsions— his conclusions are not for everyone. A
stone falls in a straight line for one. The same stone falls in a parabolic
curve for another. Why did he hold so steady in his views? My husband
taught the children. How did life come to be on Earth?— *God*, they
answered. Is there life somewhere else in the Universe?— *The Lord
God in his Threesome.* Can we communicate with the Godhead?— *Yes,
through prayer.* In this way the Universe is sacred. Who is this God
who throws a puzzle to trip us up? It's his way or no way. If only God
would share what he knows. He takes my seven sons and three daugh-
ters and puts more sons and daughters in their place. Jemima, Keziah
and Keren-happuch are the new girls' names.[21] Did he think all was
mended? I hear the cries of my first sons and daughters. The loss of
thousands of sheep, donkeys, oxen, and camels.[22] Job watches the plan-
ets through his telescope, his parchment rolled into a tube. These nights
are a field of bees. The spears of stars fall past us. This star-watcher,
this comet-man. Have you not heard? Job said to me. He walks in the

---

[21] JOB 42:14
[22] JOB 1:14–19

circuit of heaven.[23] I think of space rolled as parchment into a tube through which the planets pass. If only we were alone here— without the Watcher— the beekeeper— over us. The planets circle the sun on their course, their roll-ways, their little corridors. A children's game. But this is not a game. We are the condensation of elements from this far-off God. We live. We suffer. We are gone. What do I know of peace?

[23] JOB 22:14

PART
FOUR

THE LONG ARC OF MY DRIVING

Long passage over the land is
struggle,
it said to me.

I would not believe he listened to my voice— JOB 9:16

July 20, 2017, I drove from eastern Kansas to the Ash Hollow Historical State Park in western Nebraska to view seven Native American artifacts on loan from the Smithsonian.

I-70 west to U.S. 183 north to I-80 west to U.S. 26 west at Ogallala to the State Park, 563 miles on the long arc of my driving.

Long drives in a short time have become a means of research. My forward going on the road revealed a *backflow*— a term I found in physics meaning quantum particles can reverse and travel [partially] in a direction opposite of their momentum. I make these research trips alone. I can't be with anyone. I have to travel by myself to connect with the past.

The Battle at Ash Hollow had several names. The Harney Massacre. First Sioux War 9/2–3/1855. Blue Water Creek Battlefield, Nebraska Territory. A punitive massacre for the Grattan Massacre the year before when 30 U.S. soldiers were killed by Indians near Fort Laramie. At Ash Hollow— 85 *belligerents* were killed, 70 women and children captured, marched 140 miles to Fort Laramie. Tepees were looted. Army Lt. G.K. Warren took artifacts, gave them later to the Smithsonian. ["Artifacts that tell the story of massacre in Nebraska Territory will be displayed at state historic park," David Hendee, *The Omaha World-Herald*, 5/30/17.]

Seven of 68 artifacts donated by Lt. Warren to the Smithsonian were to be seen, to be viewed, to be returned to the place from which they came, though actually they came from Nebraska, so they would be returned to the Smithsonian where they were not from—

A beaded pouch made from the bladder of a bison, containing red-dyed and undyed porcupine quills.

A pair of moccasins made from tanned bison hide and decorated with beads and quills. At the end of the tongue are long, quill-wrapped buckskin fringes. Across the top are 12 lanes of single-quill, double-thread porcupine quill-work.

A beaded ammunition bag made of tanned bison hide and a powder horn. The pouch originally contained bullets, iron arrowheads and gunflints. The powder horn is from a domestic cow. Fur companies stocked commercially made powder horns for Indian trade.

A bow made of Osage orange. 46 inches long. The collection card states that the bow is from the Yankton Sioux, whom Lt. G.K. Warren encountered in 1855 and 1857.

A beaded rattle on a stick. The 70 rattles are aligned in three rows and made of the dew claws from the inner hooves of deer or pronghorn.

A pad saddle of dressed deer or elk skin. Decoration of floral bead-work.

A doll made of tanned leather, dress of blue wool cloth. The hair a divot of horsehide with the hair attached. Eyes and mouth are black beads. The doll wears Lakota female short leggings and moccasins.

In 1855, there was an encampment of two Lakota villages along Blue Water Creek at Ash Hollow— 40 tepees and 11 Oglala lodges. Col. William S. Harney attacked and destroyed the encampment to avenge the Indian annihilation of Lt. John Grattan's men near Fort Laramie in 1854. Lakota say that soldiers killed an Indian child wrapped in a carrier and used the body for target practice. Atrocities were not detailed in Army reports. But the voices of old battles are still on the land.

From the *Journals* of Lt. G.K. Warren—

> Wounded women and children crying and moaning, horribly mangled
> by the bullets. Most of this had been occasioned by the creatures taking
> refuge in holes in the rocks, and armed Indians sheltering themselves
> in the same places These latter fired upon our men killing 2 men &
> wounding another of the Artillery Company— Two Indian men were
> killed in the hole and two as they came out. 7 women were killed in the
> hole & 3 children, 2 of them in their mothers' arms.

After I read the article about the visit of the artifacts to Ash Hollow, I believed sometimes I heard the doll's voice. Not an audible voice, of course, but a presence that would be there. When I saw her in the case in the interpretive center, I named her *Dressed in Trophy Clothes*—

It was not the girl's mother who made the doll,
not her grandmother,
but an uncle with his knife who cut a piece of tanned hide.

The girl was not yet old enough to sew a doll
[would never be].

There were strands of horsehair on the doll's head.
A relative sewed two black beads for eyes
and two black beads for mouth.
The doll had no ears.
She was missing an arm.
The doll's dress was navy blue wool.
There was a row of blue and white beading across the shoulders of
the dress.
Around the bottom of the skirt were four narrow stripes of tan cloth.
Around her ankles, the beaded edge of her leggings.
She wore beaded moccasins.

Could she be dressed in the remnants of a U.S. military uniform?
Wasn't the beading on her shoulders epaulets?
The stripes of tan cloth from a soldier's trousers?
Did the girl's uncle cut pieces of cloth from a soldier after the Grattan
Massacre
when it was soldiers lying dead in a field?

The beads were trade beads,
but the wool cloth?

The look on the doll's face was dazed as she stared ahead.
It was as if the Harney Massacre had just happened,
and now it was the Indians a year later who were dead.
Her leather face darkened with the years.
Her other arm pulled loose in the grip of the dead girl.

America's longest war was [is] against its indigenous. Its most deadly
and brutal. Since contact, 50 to 100 million Indians have been killed
by U.S. Cavalry soldiers, and by disease and starvation because of the
loss of buffalo and other game.

There may have been between 700 and 800 tribes with as many lan-
guages. Names no longer known. Many of the Indians were primi-
tive. Without merit. Lewis & Clark made note of the disgust in their
1804–06 *Journals*. But other times, the Indians had a sense of under-
standing, compassion, wisdom, and judgment. They were as diverse
as Europeans. They had a language that surpassed English in its con-
glomeration of other languages.

A language with a land base of moving verbs—
He who is hunting.
He who is bringing game.
He who is going. [The act of motion when soldiers were arriving.]

I am driving on the road where I am going. The meaning of the journey
is in its continuum until returning to the place of departure. Winter
camp to summer camp to moving camps following the migratory buf-
falo. The artifacts from the Smithsonian traveling to Ash Hollow and
back. The absolute dependence on verbs for sustenance. Not in one

place for long. But packing up tepees, folding over hides, putting them on travois, moving on.

There were Indian wars among the Indians before contact with the European. There was cruelty. They took one another's land where they hunted, one another's wives and children. The stronger raided the weaker. They bullied. Some of it was survival. Some of it to take what others had. For the pleasure of taking. For being able to push another tribe along, if you wanted their hunting grounds. Or what they had— horses, usually, after they were taken from Spanish explorers.

After defeat by the U.S. Cavalry, the Indian was given unwanted parcels of land and told, Farm. Without knowing the concept. Those who said, Farm, were without understanding the void that farming left in a migratory tribe.

At present, some 574 tribes are recognized.

Driving across the high plains, the road ahead was in my sight as if the car were a rifle. A piece of writing is an arc. A rise in what happens. The high point which is the arc after which a falling toward the resolution. Making treaties, it is called.

But what is the arc for the American Indian story? There was a vast and different tribal inhabitation of America before it was America. A vast inhabitation after America was America. It was not a war of one tank lined up after another, but the placement of Indians on the poverty and isolation of the reservations. Or when that didn't work, the removal of them to inner cities for the Relocation Act [1956] where they were told, thrive. Or their return to the reservation when they floundered in cities. Or stayed there in isolation and poverty.

Terrain is a tract of land. From the Latin *terrenum*— piece of earth. There is rain in terrain. But not in the object the word names. Terrain in Gr.— *paursus*— meaning dry, barren. Latin— *torrere*— dry up. Old German— *thurri*— meaning the same.

An arc is a curved line.

A bow string pulled back to release an arrow driven to the point where it is going.
An arc is the band of sparks that jump between electrodes. As if a campfire on the open plains. The villages under full moonlight that lit the prairie as if it were still dusk.

The arc of the quarter moon when it was a white canoe.

The tribes on the Great Plains—
Arapaho
Cheyenne
Kansa
Missouri
Omaha
Otoe
Pawnee
Ponca
Sac & Fox
Sioux [Lakota]
Winnebago

These were the Indians there.

A narrative arc causes change. The arc in the Indian story is move-
ment from one place to another. Bringing the character to a low point.
Removing what the character depends upon [buffalo], forcing the char-
acter to new strength without former structures. As was laid out for
the American Indian to remove all tepee poles. All tepee hides painted
with exploits. And live as though the tepees were still standing.

The doll dressed in parts of an army uniform is conjecture. But the
dress looked like it was taken from an article of soldier's clothing and
redefined.

Prehistoric North American horses died out between 13,000 and 11,000
years ago during the cold that was here. They returned in the sixteenth
century on Spanish ships, though there are conflicting stories. They
could have come from China. But stone anchors found off the Palos
Verdes peninsula in southern California thought to be from ancient
China, turned out to be anchors of Monterey shale. Spain is the likely
source of the horse. They came with Spanish explorers from Mexico. In
1680, the Pueblo Revolt drove Spaniards from New Mexico Territory.
They left their horses as they fled. The sedentary Pueblos did not need
to ride horses and sold them to Apache and Navajo. Thereafter the
horse spread— to Ute and Comanche upward through the Great Plains.
The first horses were recorded in Kansas in 1745.

Lewis & Clark said the horse-collectors, the Shoshone, were raided
again and again for their horses. The explorers went to the Shoshone
for the horses they needed to cross the mountain range they knew was

ahead. They hoped for an east–west water route across the continent, but discovered there were five mountain ranges between the Missouri and Columbia rivers.

But still, the earliest Old-World horse along the West Coast of North America might have been the Chinese Bashkir. [Fragments of stories abound from somewhere—] [as a doll's dress resembles fragments of a sergeant's trousers with stripes]—

Did you get the little horses from the Vikings?
He responded, No, from the Chinese.

[sidetracked here again] Afghani monk, Hui Shen, reported he had seen horses and wagons 458–490.

Later, it is said the Chinese brought horses from China on Manila Galleons for the Franciscan Missions on El Camino Real— the high-way that connected the mission outposts from San Diego north to San Francisco. In 1623, Fray Benavides wrote in his journal that he met a band of Gila Apache with the War Chief riding a horse. In 1676, it is written that Fray Ayala went to New Spain and brought back several hundred horses.

Each horse was placed in a narrow scaffolding of four posts with beams across the top. The horses were held in the stalls, leather straps under their bellies tied to beams, feet tied fore and aft, head caught in a halter so the horse stayed upright and in place during the unsteady and often perilous ocean crossing. Their progeny, staked beside tepees, must have told one another stories of their ancestors' crossings. Their later fright at bit and rein— a *backflow* to the ocean voyage held tight in a stall.

Thus, the North American horse came from several places, which always is what history is about as its opposing origins move and arc over the unknown and back, bunked and debunked and bunked again, with information sleeping on top of other information, or under it, as happened in the bunkhouse of history.

There were folds and creases on the land along the North Platte River as I drove east on U.S. 26 toward 1-80 back to Kansas. There were large, wide fields mowed of hay between the hills, the tan stripes from mowing similar to the stripes on a soldier's trousers— or the skirt of a Lakota doll's dress. It was an American landscape of minimalism. A meaning of distance.

By 12:30 p.m., July 21, 2017, it was 100°.

What was it that spoke as I drove from Ash Hollow in Nebraska? The wind? The resistance of the car to the wind? The voices of settlers who struggled— forging creeks and rivers— taking weeks to cross land that I had crossed in a few hours in my car on the interstate? Ash Hollow was a grove of ash trees in a low place between the hills— a stopover on the Oregon / California trails. Wagon ruts were still visible on the land. There had been rope-scars on an old tree stump that acted as a windlass to let the wagons down the steep incline as the westward movement moved westward across the terrain.

At Ash Creek Hollow, Col. Harney had divided his troops, leading his infantry across the North Platte while other troops circled from another direction. Harney met Little Thunder, chief of the Sicangu band of the Lakota, and asked for the braves in the Grattan Massacre. Little Thunder refused to name them. Harney told him to prepare for a fight, and the infantry opened fire, forcing the Indians toward the mounted soldiers.

A doll missing one arm belonging to a dead Lakota girl was taken from the battlefield by Lt. Warren to be preserved in the Smithsonian, her little voice like the squeak of a bird in a distant juniper bush.

As I returned to Kansas, I listened to a CD of the Book of Job.

I am full of tossings— JOB 7:4
I will speak to the anguish in my spirit— JOB 7:11
How long will you not look away nor leave me alone until I swallow my spit— JOB 7:19
Why do you set a mark against me until I am a burden to myself— JOB 7:20

It could have been a litany from the Journals of Lt. G.K. Warren— the lines of Job transposed on the Ash Hollow Battlefield. The suffering Job. The grieving Lt. Warren over the atrocities he witnessed. The decimated villages of the Lakota as Col. Harney and his troops sought revenge for the murdered soldiers the previous year. The desolation of the Lakota survivors as they were marched from their land to Fort Laramie, if they survived the 140-mile march. They would become Indians known as *hang-around-the-fort*, meaning they would be dependent on others for sustenance.

All this in Job because God made a bet with Satan in the opening chapter?

Were God and Satan not above sparring?

The Book of Job is a long journey. A road that opens before the car traveling there. A road that seems to drive through Native history. A doll dressed in trophy clothes. A God who clothed Job in trouser stripes and dark blue wool cloth— saying to Satan, My weapons are bigger than yours. God the U.S. military. Satan the Indians. Though the perspective would be reversed from a reversed perspective of the Indians.

I drove I-80 east across Nebraska to U.S. 81 south to I-70 east. By 5:00 p.m., it was 108°. At 5:30, the dashboard thermometer read, 109°.

On a bluff above the North Platte River at the Ash Hollow Historical State Park, I had picked up a flat bottom pebble for a totem. I have a collection of small rocks in nearly every room in my house, some in baskets, some on the wood floor. I have a small shadow box which holds favored stones. They are different shapes of igneous, sedimentary, meta-morphic. They are journals of my goings and comings along many trails, gravel roads, dirt roads, back roads, and highways, some of which are now called interstates. The rocks come from the long journeys I have made for research. Mainly historical sites in America's longest war. I don't think I could travel without their voices.

In two days, I drove 1,211 miles, returning to where I was from. The night was so quiet after the journey, I could hear the stars.

PART
FIVE

ABSTRACT

Job's wife is moved to share her sewing basket as she considers the travels of Brevet General George Custer from North Dakota into Montana

Questionings ^ argumentations ^ laments ^ conjectures ^ earlier Indian wars ^ the appropriation of scholarship by poetry

Key Words
Fabric ^ [text] isle ^ a line of horses ^ between the curtains ^ of the upstairs officer's quarters ^ Middle English *ile* ^ Vulgar Latin *isula* ^ Latin *insula*

Her isle in the waves of prairie grass ^ until the general returns on his horse ^ threads running from the guillotine of scissors coming

A show [-down] ^ hoe [-down] ^ needles with the tiniest rip at the top ^ spools and thimbles ^ various ways two wives are similar in warp and weft

UNTIL THE TIMES OF RESTITUTION— ACTS 3:21

Jung thought Indians thought trees talked, skies moved because of vacuousness. A primitive, as one not yet conscious of the place of self in the world. As someone who didn't keep their doors locked. There was a time anyone could walk in. Even without knocking.

Knockers were used by Anishinaabe to knock rice into the canoe. Everyone has their own version of knocking. I could be excluded. As if forthwith I was not a part of enduring. For Job, it was three men who knocked at his door.

Another way to say it. A man from Uz suffered the loss of children in a storm. Tribal in that the animals suffered with him. His herds— sheep, camel, ox, donkey— taken. The others— goat, peacock, ostrich, hawk, horse, leviathan, behemoth. All of them found in his book. Ask the animals and they will teach you, the birds in the sky. Let fish declare— JOB 12:7–8.

Job sat with friends who were not friends. As loose threads on a tunic. A robe or whatever Job wore to cover boils and knots in his thoughts. To ponder his situation. A forerunner for the Indian who lost his place and was made to sit and receive tripe from his visitors.

PRETEND

To cause or attempt to cause what is not so to seem to be so. From the Middle English *pretenden*, the French *prétendre*, the Latin *praetendere*, to stretch forth [the feet to run] to stretch in front of. I also saw the word, perfidious, while looking, which can be another form of pretending.

The squeaking of these words past their meanings. A pretend face in a papier-mâché mask or the mask of the Lone Ranger.

Maybe it was in grade school pretending to be a cowboy or an Indian scout. Could it be confused with someone not playing though they pretended to play oboe or cello or piano until they stopped practicing?

A verb when it is transitive may take a clause as object to make believe, as in, you pretend you receive a letter from Crazy Horse. An intransitive presents a claim [especially dubious], you pretend to read.

It was correct. I did not know the culture directly. It was subsumed into us who were among others who lived apart from them. I knew when visiting the pow-wow or traditional ceremonies, I am not one of these.

This correspondence from Crazy Horse is likewise pretend. As my great-grandfather pretended it was not him who ran from trouble and covered his trail and himself, but word got out he wasn't who he seemed.

You know Crazy Horse never spoke to me. We were of different worlds that did not overlap. I could not see him, but waited for him to write.

I answered other letters and tended the row of beans at the back door until his letters came—

I saw the soldiers ride from Fort Phil Kearney. They were woodcutters harassed by Indians. They made it back to the fort, but Fetterman and soldiers rode after us. None of them returned.[24]

I am reluctant to tell you the disaster that met the soldiers. The land was ours in the 1851 Laramie Treaty. It was written on the paper. But they went on as they did. Were we to believe the treaty and blind ourselves to their continual passing through our hunting grounds? No matter— let wagon train after wagon train pass. We should look upon them as not passing. It is written in words that no wagon trains pass. They only pretended to be there?

Therefore, all the soldiers returned to the fort. We did not kill them. Strip them. Mutilate them. We did not use ambush or decoy to lure them farther then they could return— de [the] kooi [cage] from the Dutch. As nets around a marsh trap waterfowl.

[The gin shall take him by the heel . . . the snare is laid for him in the ground, and a trap for him in the way— JOB 18:9–10]

I use the soldiers' words the way they use them. All your soldiers returned to Fort Phil Kearny, December 21, 1866, in the Battle of the

---

[24] On December 21, 1866, Crazy Horse and six other warriors including Red Cloud decoyed Captain William Fetterman's infantrymen into ambush. All 81 men were killed by the Lakota, Cheyenne, and Arapaho. The Battle of the Hundred-in-Hands is also known as the Fetterman Massacre.

Hundred-in-the-Hands [retaliation for Sand Creek[25]]. We do not know what was on the ground with arrows sticking up like stalks in a field. We follow what you taught us. Ride into the blizzard to collect the frozen bodies we say are not there.

It is our treaty pretending to be a treaty with words that have no meaning full of flying particles in the storm of this every day we have every day happening.

[25] Also known as the Chivington Massacre. November 29, 1864, 675 men of the Third Colorado Cavalry under the Command of U.S. Army Colonel John Chivington destroyed a village of Cheyenne and Arapaho, killing between 70 and 500, many of whom were women and children.

AN ORDINARY DAY TO WORK

I like books because they have covers.
What they are is inside.

His bestiary pillaged.
He had nothing on his plate in Uz.
His sorrow buzzed.
Have you spoken to the camels?
They are gone.
The hippopotamus and oxen?
Gone also.
Sons and daughters?
Taken by a storm.
Was ransom given?
No— he wrote in his day book—
The storm does not leave notes.
Have you spoken to the sheep?
They are not there either to speak.
The mules? Hawk? Gazelle?
The grouse along the fence that creep?
Nothing there
not even louse.

THE SO-CALLED OSTRICH SPEECH[26]

Was her there just once
doing faith the Book of Job is about?
Scholars say the ostrich is a mistranslation
of the Hebrew *mynnr*
and is a coroneted sandgrouse
or singed [chestnut-bellied] grouse
or spotted grouse
or pin-tailed, black-bellied grouse.
Ostrich: What grouse could outrun horse?
No this is what is soup.
The inner brain of Job was suffering lack of faith—
let there be darkness.
Is the ostrich a bird?
Ostrich: Yes— a giraffe of a bird.
Earthbound, I regret.
What God would make a flightless bird
to carry these heavy wings about?—
yet when horses run I overtake
forgetting hatchlings buried in the desert sand
as Job lost sight at first of faith
more thinking about losing his post in Uz
than hatching new wisdom and
understanding to lift up feather-brained
bird-brained Job
for the purpose in his trials.

[26] JOB 39:13–18

HE LIVETH

Were it a whale, the sea had bounds.
But not suffering.
Job lost all.
His friends went bazooka with accusations.

If Job did not understand at first
then who, I ask, could understand God
who would brag to Satan
who in turn would say, give Job to me and see
the stuffing in the overstuffed benefactor
who fed orphans and widows and was benevolent
to the nth degree in chapter 29th.
The self-sung Job and all he did and was in Uz.

It was there at midnight I found the exit
to Walmart off Interstate 35 in Wichita
where I waited out the storm
in my car until light.

I know my redeemer liveth, and that he shall stand
at the latter day upon the earth.[27]

And thus it was in the deepest bite of rain
that sadness was a perpendicular line
upright to heaven

[27] JOB 19:25

because of Job's sorrow and restoration
I could handle the benefits of God
working on things until I came forth
through loss with more than in the beginning.
A shape in the ball of suffering
like that in the furnace, but none were burned.

HE HAVE NOTHING TO DO THE REST
OF THE DAY BUT JUMPING

It was at first doubtable
ox and donkey taken by Sabeans
sheep burned in fire-ball from God
[or so the servant called it]
camels taken by Chaldeans
children killed in whirlwind
[I only am escaped alone to tell thee]
who could believe
God's grace was sufficient
but Job
force-marched through disaster
to get past his own thinking
into God's portal
I have seen
I will see again
there faith documented by suffering
opens the wound of self-satisfaction sitting at the head
of the gate of Uz
who at last can say
faith is buried in trials
even the most stunning.

LEAVE THE WIFE ALONE LET HER FIRE UP HER TOASTER

For a longhorn
she kept a bicycle-seat for a head
handlebars for horns.

The boys' old bicycles taken apart
dismantled for soot.

At the smoldering trash pile
the rubber burning
or was it the buttering of the bread for the toaster?

THE TAKEN PARTS OF A TEXT.

[Know.] Nelly Don [1889–1991] sold housedresses in stores and catalog-ordered from Kansas City. [ ] not willing to hang itself as if [ ] a closet pole. Threads drawn by pulling them. The [ ] of peplum over skirt. Never shiny in the seat when worn. The military wife on out[post]— your order has shipped— [North Dakota— Fort Lincoln]. An ironing board put down for a bridge. Day dresses with funnel cuffs. Soutache-rimmed collar. Dolman sleeves. Pannier gathered at sides. [Double row of stitching around the waist] to let out if long-waist[ed]. [75 million Nelly Don dresses sold— 1916–1978.] House dresses in floral and patterned print [sheep] [little camels on lapel]. If I wash myself with snow water— JOB 9:30. [Nelly never sold her fabrics by the yard, which her successors did— and soon closed down the line.] Job's wife— 10 wraparound aprons [patent filed April 3, 1925] for [self] and kitchen servants. A thicket of [garden] herbs. Boarded windows— [the field servant's quarters.] Bowls to wash. Shadows moving along the stone-piled wall.

CLARIFICATION FOR THE KNITTING AND FABRIC-ARTS CLUB OF UZ

Burl

[noun]
 1. a small knot or lump in wool / in thread /
in cloth
 2. a gnarl on the trunk of a tree
a large rounded outgrowth developed when the bud
of a twig does not grow outward into a limb but
sticks close to the tree

[verb]
 1. to remove a burl from cloth [i.e. burl the burl]

[misc.]
 1. burl also means attempt

Purl

[noun]
 1. a backward stitch in knitting—
Knit one purl one
Cast 35 stitches upon each of three needles
and knit around 30 times in single rib—

that is, knit 1, purl 1, alternately—
Handbook of Wool Knitting and Crochet, Anonymous]

[verb]

    1. to put a knitting needle through the front
of the stitch from right to left

[misc.]

    1. early 16th-century word meaning stream or river
[a flowing swirling motion] [as knitting often is]

BRIDGE[28]

and abundance of water covers thee— JOB 22:11

How would Job cross the water in Uz if the river was not dry? Weren't there travels with 3,000 camels among his sheep oxen asses? Did the camels caravan? Or did Job leave them chewing in his pastures? Or did he rent the camels to others? Job was a rich man. Commerce must have been on his mind. Did he use the camels to take his bundles of wool to market? His crops? Was Uz far from his hacienda? Were there other places he sold his goods? Maybe he sent his servants with the camels on long journeys. Maybe he sent his sons. Were there camel-trains as there are now campers, RVs, a bridge across the river to try? Was he thinking how to use the bridge to travel to where and what for? With all their words as a bridge across the shores of a story. O that one might plead for a man with God— JOB 16:21. His longing for a daysman as Savior between them. The thought with always a way across the water.

---

[28] From the root *bhru* [log, beam], Old English *brycge*, Old Germanic *brugjo*, Old Saxon *bruggia*, Old Norse *bryggja*, Old Dutch *brug*, Old *brucca* or Old *brucke*. How language like bridges developed.

HOW CAN I KEEP FROM HAPPENING THIS?

Where were you when I shut the sea
with doors when it broke loose?
When I said, you can go this far
and no farther.
Do you see yourself as waves at all?
A leader in your city
with indignation for its outcasts.
Have you rowed your dinghy
across the water?
Have you searched the depth?
Declare if you know all.
Have you entered the storehouse
of the hail or snow—
or frost, for that matter?
Do you know the ordinances anywhere?
Where is the way where light dwells?
And as far as darkness
where is its place?
The clamoring city. A storm of traffic
on the clogged interstate. The off-
beat dwellers— maybe even gypsies
in Uz— [or Indians]— not wanted.
You downsized them with your words.
I say I was nowhere— Job answered.
I have borne chastisement
I will not any more offend.

It is a humbling place— this wrong-
headedness always seen too late
to change or undo what has been done.
O bristling heart.
I was not fair to them while I learned
the diversity of a viable city.

THE QUESTIONING

I perched on your highest bird—
Paradelle for Susan, BILLY COLLINS

Can you draw out leviathan with a hook?— JOB 41:1
Can you draw out leviathan with a hook?— JOB 41:1
Will you play with him as with a bird?— JOB 41:5
Will you play with him as with a bird?— JOB 41:5
Leviathan?— can you draw Job a bird with hook
as you play him without a will?— JOB 41:1 41:5

What does will matter to God who calls the shots?
What does will matter to God who calls the shots?
What answer for Job other than to relinquish will?
What answer for Job other than to relinquish will?
Will God answer for the shots— other than to Job
who calls to relinquish what matter does to will?

Do why therefore and wherewith matter? Unless—
Do why therefore and wherewith matter? Unless—
By giving up smaller— greater understanding received?
By giving up smaller— greater understanding received?
Why do smaller matter wherewith received?— giving
therefore larger— unless greater by understanding up?

Therefore you with smaller bird— JOB 41:5— received
will as leviathan? A matter with a hook. Why draw
with him?— JOB 41:1. What other answer can? Unless
God relinquish play? To will and do by greater than?
For wherewith shots to Job does what?— You who
will the matter out— calls giving understanding up?

LAMENT FOR THE ANIMALS

The oxen were plowing and the asses feeding beside them: and the Sabeans fell upon them, and took them away; they have slain the servants and only I am escaped alone to tell thee. While he was speaking, there came also another, and said, The fire of God is fallen from heaven, and has burned up the sheep, and the servants, and consumed them; and I only am escaped alone to tell thee. While he was speaking, there came also another, and said, The Chaldeans fell upon the camels, and have carried them away, and slain the servants with the edge of the sword; and I only am escaped alone to tell thee— JOB 1:14–17

500 yoke of oxen, 500 asses,
7,000 sheep, 3,000 camels—
The servants with them? Gone?? How did a fire
burn 7,000 sheep? No one left to rake
the ashes. Neighbors came to bury servants in a pit.
Over there— I said— the edge of the field.

Not where I can see it— farther yet across the field.
I cry for sheep, camels, the yoke of oxen, asses.
I should grieve for the servants in the pit.
They sheared the sheep and drove the camels
with their burdens of undyed wool. I rake
the knotty field of bone fragment from the fire.

I find a tooth or two. My hands feel they are on fire.
I cannot shake the grief, but pour my tears on sodden field
as if the clouds, the thunder, and the lightning rake.
Three friends are here. I would rather have asses,
7,000 sheep, the yoke of oxen, and the camels
strolling across the desert with servants risen from the pit.

It is myself who cannot rise from the pit.
I think of innocent sheep on fire.
The yoke of oxen driven far. The camels
bellowing at the pace. Why didn't I hear the field-
dogs bark? The servants yelling out. The asses
braying. Their hooves as pitchfork and rake

against the road. Their imagined voices still rake
my ears— with voices of the servants from the pit.
What will camels and oxen do without the asses
that guard their young from wolves that roam, but not the fire?
The horses sleep, standing in the shade of the field.
Don't the doofuses know the others are gone— the camels

who were their friends, not there? I see the camels
bearing the burden of the stars when I rake
the night sky over the still-smoldering field.
I would send my three friends to the pit.
The dialogue stokes what I feel of the fire.
If they could know the yoke of oxen. The asses.

Take the rest of nothing— camels, oxen, the pit
of loss. Eat burnt grass. The rake and hay-roll. The fire.
Wallow in the field. Mourn the stars. The scrabble game. The asses.

THERE WAS IN UZ

—a cento from JOB, *chapters 29 and 30*

I delivered the poor that cried
and the fatherless
and him that had none to help.
I was eyes to the blind and feet to the lame.
I was father to the poor.
The cause I knew not I searched out.
My root was spread out by the water.
The dew lay all night on my branch.
Men kept silent at my counsel—
their tongue cleaved
to the roof of their mouth.
Justice was my robe.
I broke the jaws of the wicked
and plucked the prey from their teeth.
Now they hold me in derision whose fathers
I would have disdained to set with dogs.
They were driven from among men
to dwell in clefts, in caves and rocks.
They cut up mallows and juniper roots
for their meat.
Among the bushes they brayed
and under nettles they gathered.

They were children of fools,
children of base men.
They were viler than the earth.[29]

---

[29] Yikes— there it is. Unlike the impenetrable leviathan, Job is de-scaled. He thought himself a righteous man, yet his trials uncover the shortcomings in his snipish [and arrogant] attitude.

So where is the island of the innocent? A leader in Uz who heard of God with his ears, and who suffered until he saw God with his eyes— JOB 42:5? The innocent are those who have faith? Those who recognize their humanity? Belief is the island of the innocent? Or belief in the manifold possibilities and multiple understandings of the world?

FLUVIAL

Did they work together— the Sabeans and
Chaldeans— when they took the animals?
How many nights they waited?
The Sabeans tripping over their long feet
the hem of their robes
the head-wraps as they came unrolled.
Those Chaldeans with horses faster than eagles
warriors ruffians
loose on the land always moving— they jump the tracks.
How long it take to put themselves together?
Didn't the puppers bark?
Why not I wake?—
Indecisive grumbling herds.
I would send the field servants after them
[if I had them]
[but they too were killed]
The enclosures [ ] [ ] empty.
The bodies left in the field for us to bury.
House servants— all I have.
No, bring the tractor from the barn.
They could never dig [not used to field work— to anything
but peeling collards].
The slow plod of camels.
Of driving donkeys and 500 yoke of oxen
[1,000 on my *go-count*]
If Fussell could find the wood-stove with his armload of wood—

the chicken in diablo sauce the black beans.

The Sabeans took the donkeys [she-asses] and oxen.

The Chaldeans got the camels.

Did they open the gates?— hold a bucket before the animals

call from the desert

here the streams flow.

HE DRESSED ME FOR THE PRETEND COLD

The camels of Bildad, Zophar, Eliphaz in the pasture. It was empty after Job's camels were taken. They always had talked. But now they picked up on the emptiness. They wedged against the fence as though to feel solid against the open. They stood with one another as they once stood together against the herd of another whose pasture they were in. The servants there. The camel herders to keep them from harm. With sticks they said you here. You there. But the camels had intermixed. Now there was nothing but air to mix with. If others were taken could they be taken too? Was that the feeling they felt? Where had 3,000 camels gone? They ate the grass of camels who were not there. They had ownership now. A breaking and entering of sorts. As when passing other camel trains in the desert. The knowing they were with men who let them pass. Now it was left to them to stand in the pasture backed into their own unintelligence of all that passed. They only had to step into the wide pasture. The nothingness. It was slow in coming. The train you hear at night pass all the way through town. Its horn at every corner.

PART
SIX

I know that Thou canst do every thing,
and that no thought can be withholden from Thee—
JOB 42:2

AN ACT OF INVASION

When he asked me for a snappy title I sent him— Let Her Fire Up Her
Toaster: the Reaction of Job and His Wife to Suffering

A man and his wife caught in difficult circumstances— heated up as if
between the coils of a toaster.

The reasons for suffering—
Suffering uncovers the mystery of who one is. What is inside.

Job's sufferings, allowed by God, opened Job's eyes to himself—
Job realized he was a self-satisfied, humanitarian snob who finally saw
his meagerness before God.
There was an attitude that needed to be dealt with.
Job deals and finally says, Therefore, I abhor myself, and repent in dust
and ashes— JOB 42:6.

Even in the depth of his suffering, the Job that would come forth as
gold was there, buried in the rubble of his thoughts that suffering would
make him aware of—
He knoweth the way that I take; when he hath tried me, I shall come
forth as gold— JOB 23:10.

The same thought appears in the New Testament—
But the God of all grace, who hath called us unto his eternal glory by
Christ Jesus, after ye have suffered awhile, make you perfect, establish,

strengthen, settle you. To him be glory and dominion forever and ever. Amen— I PETER 5:10–11.

Perfect here means complete— as Job was complete when he said, after his trials, I have heard of thee by the hearing of the ear, but now mine eye seeth thee.

Do you want to know more of me? God seems to ask at times. It will take a crushing of the human ego.

If we suffer we should reign with him— II TIMOTHY 2:12.

In the world you will have tribulation— JOHN 16:33.

Romans 8:18–19, 22— I reckon that the sufferings of this present time are not worthy to be compared with the glory which shall be revealed in us. For the earnest expectation of the creation waits for the manifestation of the sons of God.
For we know that the whole creation groans and travails in pain together until now.

II CORINTHIANS 1:5— For as the sufferings of Christ abound in us, so our consolation also aboundeth in Christ.

II CORINTHIANS 1:7— As ye are partakers of the sufferings, so shall ye be also of the consolation.

PHILIPPIANS 3:10— That I may know him, and the power of his resurrection, and the fellowship of his suffering, being made conformable unto his death.

I PETER 1:6–7— In this ye greatly rejoice, though now for a season, if need be, ye are in heaviness through manifold trials, That the trial of your faith, being much more precious than of gold that perisheth, though it be tried with fire, might be found unto praise and honor and glory at the appearing of Jesus Christ.

I PETER 4:13— But rejoice, inasmuch as ye are partakers of Christ's sufferings, that, when his glory shall be revealed, ye may be glad also with exceeding joy.

Job's trials continue in the New Testament in the experience of the suffering of the apostles—

And by the hands of the apostles were many signs and wonders wrought among the people . . . And believers were the more added to the Lord, multitudes both of men and women, insomuch they brought forth the sick into the streets, and laid them on beds and couches, that at the least the shadow of Peter passing by might overshadow some of them. There came a multitude out of the cities round about unto Jerusalem bringing sick folks, and them who were vexed with unclean spirits; and they were healed every one. Then the high priest rose up, and all they that were with him . . . and laid their lands on the apostles, and put them in the common prison. But an angel of the Lord by night opened the prison doors, and brought them forth, and said, Go, stand and speak in the temple to the people all the words of this life— from Acts 5:12–20
Then went the captain with the officers, and brought them without violence; for they feared the people, lest they should have been stoned. And when they brought them, they set them before the council, and the high priest asked them, saying, Did not we strictly command that

ye should not teach in this name? And behold, ye have filled Jerusalem with your doctrine— ACTS 5:26–28.

And when they had called the apostles, and beaten them, they commanded that they should not speak in the name of Jesus, and let them go. And they departed from the presence of the council, rejoicing that they were counted worthy to suffer shame for his name— ACTS 5:40–41.

Paul lists his sufferings—

II CORINTHIANS 11:25–27— Thrice I was beaten with rods, once I was stoned, thrice I suffered shipwreck, a night and a day I have been in the deep; In journeyings often, in perils of waters, in perils of robbers, in perils by mine own countrymen, in perils by the heathen, in perils in the city, in perils in the wilderness, in perils in the sea, in perils among false brethren; In weariness and painfulness, in watching often, in hunger and thirst, in fastings often, in cold and nakedness.

Job also listed his sufferings— in perils of the Sabeans, three bands of Chaldeans, fire and wind, the loss of children, and the accusations of friends, the physical pain of boils— and the harrowing peril of Job himself when he recognized his unworthiness before God. Without suffering for that purpose, Job would have remained a lesser man of God.

Job's story is tidy. He suffered. He saw an underlying reason God put him through his trials. He came out tried as gold. His life and possessions were restored.

But it is Job's wife also who interests me.

When I thought of her in the scaffolding the Bible sometimes presents, I imagined her narrative. I didn't see the ultimate moment for her that

Job had— [now I see God]. I think Jehorah represents the times we suffer and don't understand why. If she is not the main character in the drama that Job is, she stands worthy between the coils of the toaster.

I, JOB

The Forge of the Heart, 1529

[The smallest engraving in the gallery—
hardly a finger's-width on the wall.]

The design of this engraved bookplate was probably conceived by
Nuremberg's leading classical scholar, Willibald Pirckheimer [1470–
1530]. The central image is an allegory that urges patience during
trying times. Female personifications of Tribulation and Envy
hammer at an anvil that bears Pirckheimer's coat of arms, a birch tree.
Tolerance shoulders the brunt of this assault with great composure.
Hope offers comfort by pointing to the rain shower that provides the
flaming heart with relief.

In the tumbling of all that came down
there was light.
I knew it. Insisted on it
despite three friends drilling their accusations
into my head.
I am innocent, you morons.

They sit at my hacienda eating tilapia and baked cauliflower
in my wife's gasparillo sauce,
[or whatever those green pellets are called].

The flames that—
quickly quickly, I think—
burned up the sheep—
I could not bear it otherwise—
[that they suffered].
They seemed dumb, but if a lamb was removed,
taken to market or butchered behind their back,
the mother grieved for days,
baah-ing at the emptiness.
What do we know of animals—
of their patience during suffering?

Why didn't the servants protect the herds
when Sabeans came for the 500 yoke of oxen and 500 asses,
and Chaldeans took the 3,000 camels?

The capers of enemies and friends— what grace is that?—
[that's what those green pellets are called].

The camels are stubborn and do not move without prodding.
How did they get the whole herd to move?

Tribulation pounds my heart.
I envy the friends who sit upright before me,
no boils or loss of all they own.

DRIVING THROUGH SNOW ACROSS OHIO, JANUARY 12, 2018

It was the crows I remember in Pittsburgh
circling above the trees
before the cold snap that was coming—
below zero the forecast.
They knew also in their long journey of survival
searching roofs for chimneys— heat vents—
a ripple in the cold air that meant heat.
How does a flock get through unbearable cold
gripped tight as a claw around a branch?
The hammer-stone of cold asserting itself
in the spill of morning light into evening darkness—
the crows still circling as if catching strands of air
to pull into a tight bag around the trees
in which they could ride the galloping storm wind—
as if a gathering of circus clowns
in a 20-cent movie in some remote long-ago town.
The marquee of winter clouds coming
as the next attraction.
Their eye on what would move across the screen
of the movie theater
they only watched and were not in.

UNDERNOTE: It was a bitter two weeks in Pittsburgh during the MFA low-residency program at Carlow University. It had been 1° when I left Kansas on December 31st. –4° when I left Richmond, Indiana, on the Ohio border January 1st. It was not a hard drive— 840 miles— Kansas City, St. Louis, Indianapolis, Columbus, Pittsburgh— there it was –7° and colder. The crows circled the trees outside Aquinas Hall. The question was— how do the birds and animals survive?— the rocks— the trees— the circle of the sky? What invisible means do they have to outlast the cold? What small, inner furnace do they turn on? I wondered how to circle the enclosure of the poem and also find an escape route.

WHAT SHE COOKED IN WHITE LARD
ON THE WOOD STOVE.

What she cooked was the chicken she chopped the head off of.
What she cooked was the chicken that flopped after it was beheaded.
What she cooked was the chicken whose head was left for the crows
or slop for the pigs— its eye a portal to the sky.
What she cooked was the chicken whose feathers she plucked until
her hands were a cluster of small white leaves.

UNDERNOTE: It was the farm the farm the farm of my grandparents. My
mother's parents. 69 miles south on highway 69 from Kansas City to the
farm near Prescott, Kansas. It was a long trip in those days on a single-lane
highway through Louisburg and Pleasanton and Prescott to the left turn off
the highway at the curve. The car slowing to hit the gravel of the farm-road
that curved once and once again. The rise of dust behind the car. The gravel
rattling under the car. The slowing at a crossroad with its blind corners
because of tall weeds or brush at the edge of fields. The further slowing of
the car as it turned into the wheel-ruts over the drainage ditch into the drive-
way of the farmhouse, staunch, white, plain, enduring. The barn and sheds.
The chicken coop. The clucking. The little fenced chicken yard locked for
the night against predators. I stood back from watching as she came with
the chicken upside-down flapping its wings as she held its legs tightly. And
quickly put its neck on the stump and took the ax swiftly across its neck.
Still holding the chicken that continued to flop without its head. Blood run-
ning from its neck— holding it— still holding it— until the wings stopped
flapping. Further down highway 69 was Fort Scott where the husband of an

aunt was from. On the farm— the little forts of chicken coop and farmhouse against the open prairie. The soldier-hens on guard against the fox. The snake. The sense that some were disappearing.

WHERE DOES THE RIVER GO AT NIGHT?

They started with everything packed
but rattled loose

shaken came apart turned over
uprighted again

and then with what was left
to see at night the point

they started from that morning
the going as if slow motion

as if now in circles while loss
goes by straight.

A CONTROLLED BURN

The fire of God is fallen from heaven
and burned up the sheep, and the servants— JOB 1:16

When she fed the chickens
their feathers caught the edges of flame.

The servants and the remnants of sheep buried
in the smoldering field.

When you are where you don't want to be.
But R.

A similitude in loss of all that was.
Or nearly all. Was.

His wife had no defense except
to offer him supper.

The smell of charred fields
in the evening wind.

Of cost to make known. His ledger books
intact. Updated each day.

Above the escarpment the winter trees.
A gravel pit. The land of. Uz.

THERE IS JOB IN HIS YARD CHAIR.

He sits in discomfort before his three friends. It is worthy of portraiture. Eliphaz in a blue robe. Bildad in brown. Zophar in gray. An orange leaf has fallen on Bildad's shoulder. An Araucana of Job's wife pecking in the backyard. Job swats the low branches of a tree on the portico. Another orange leaf falls on the blue hen. The friends have paused a moment, but are anxious to speak again. For now, it is the chatter of birds. The clucking hen.

Even the women cooking supper are quiet. Once in a while, Job's wife is heard directing the servants here and there. If there had been music of any sort. But none of them could play anything.

Seven sons and three daughters gone. Oxen, asses, sheep, and camels gone. Field implements blown across the road. Hay wagons overturned. Irises would have bloomed but they were empty stalks. Even the hen seemed concerned. Much of the debris had been cleared by whatever servants were left. A pile of limbs pulled behind the hacienda to be chopped and stacked— and some of them burned when the wind was right. The awnings over the portico were crooked. The servants had not had time to straighten them yet. Maybe one of the support poles was broken. Maybe they were ripped someplace Job had not yet discovered. Job's words had blown away, too. His anger over his friends smoldered. The storm left moles and rats. Most of them. [Just out of the frame.] But there was not a sheep to sacrifice. Not a sheep to kill.

YET TROUBLE CAME

The day is hard.
A vase of smoke from the chimney of the farmhouse.
A burst of iris on the table.

How many got to the edge of land?
And wagons got them farther.
The oars of them set against the side of the barn.

Who do you say I am?— MARK 8:29—
he asked beside the nave.
The image of the early church was a ship.

The prairie a sea.
What more could be hoped?
Can the rush grow up without the mire?— JOB 8:11

DEAR GENERAL

But now I have a burning desire—
"To a Thunder Cloud,"
Yellow Bird (John Ridge)
ARKANSAS STATE GAZETTE, *January 9, 1847*

I am here [darling]
waiting at the outpost
between what is there
between us.
I am beside U as a leaf beside a tree
raked in a pile
blown by wind
I am crumbled to pieces
U can find anywhere.

YOU HAVE HEARD OF THE PATIENCE
OF JOB– JAMES 5:11

It wasn't that way. I paced the land. Bellowed at the fields.
Long suffering it was. If that's what patience means.

Barns sheds trees cows horses chickens the sky clouds stars all
those beings asked why the darkness of suffering.

Even the moon hid its light.
Behold the moon it shineth not— JOB 25:5. At night the animals

could not find their way to the barn.
I was a register of complaints. No one would listen.

I was not used to irrelevancy. The yellow farm a map.
Ruptured. It would be words that recharged a turnaround.

A language not given to loss. The moon a bulk in the sky
until caught in the turbulence of gravity, it gradually rounded.

At first a moth with spots.
The acrobat lighted the earth at night. Snake-oil it was.

The horses cows sat at their little chairs and tables.
The chickens in their smallest barn.

PART
SEVEN

For the thing which I greatly feared is come upon me, and that which I was afraid of is come unto me.
I was not in safety, neither had I rest, neither was I quiet; yet trouble came—
JOB 3:25–26

JOB IN THE INTERSTICE I

What exactly did Job fear?

He was used to his place in Uz and the certainty of his own way of thinking. Now he had come to a place where other possibilities hovered. The drone of them in his thoughts all day.

Otherness crept into his situation. He knew the accusations of his friends were off. But Job felt fissures begin to form. No, they had been there— He was just now feeling them.

Was that a possibility?— Could the definite Job keep going with no definite meaning? No definity— but that is not a word.

There are interstices between places. Unclarities— another word that is not a word.

What exactly did Job fear?— He answers himself in Job 10:22— A land of darkness, as darkness itself; and of the shadow of death, without any order, where the light is as darkness.

It was the possibility of uncertainty that interrupted truth as Job saw it. It was the possibility of other possibilities that diffused meaning Job was certain of— that cracked open Job's certain world.

It is what Native Americans feared as they saw the encroachment of the Europeans. It is what I fear in the political upheaval that threatens the foundation of the country I know.

Maybe Job feared this otherness also. This multivalent world of relativity. Without any order. Shifting. Changing. Becoming skewed. We think the world should be as we think it should be. We want God to be in our image.

Carl Jung thought that God sent Jesus to the earth because he [God] wanted to be a man. God was envious of man and guilty of his treatment of Job— causing Job to suffer unfairly.

It is the interstice that allows interpretation.

Job is in a morass. He grieves the loss of his children. He is burning with boils, head to foot. He receives scorn wherever he turns.

But in the muddle a certainty emerges.

If I justify myself, my own mouth shall condemn me; if I say, I am perfect, he shall also prove me perverse— JOB 9:20.

For he is not a man, as I am, that I should answer him, and we should come together in judgment. Neither is there any daysman between us, that might lay his hand upon us both— JOB 9:32–33.

The wretchedness of Job's suffering has brought a greater wretchedness— the realization that Job is separated from God at present— and for now, his existence is contingent on the benevolence of a God who at present is torturing him.

The daysman is not named by name, but whose name later is Christ, the one there from the beginning [as Christians believe]— present with Job, yet not known— but Job's belief that he is— or could be— is counted as righteousness.

This certainty in uncertainty. This dividing of all that he was and is and will come to understand. It is never our way after all before the living Lord.

Thus, the mystery of existence is to be feared. How easy to miss the fulcrum of life— where shall we spend the rest of it?— after our life on earth has passed.

Not even knowing we are to reach for the ring as the merry-go-round goes around and around again. To accept Christ is eternal life [Christians believe].

And worse, this after-existence is based on God who can seem irrelevant to the world as it goes by— and by— not always paying attention. Acting as if it could act on its own— yet I put my trust in this so-called [by-the-world] irrelevancy.

JOB IN THE INTERSTICE II

Job is at his hacienda. The three friends arrive thereafter. How long did Job suffer on his own before he suffered with his friends? How long did he suffer during their visit?

There seems to be an uncertainty in the time-line in Job—
Now when Job's three friends heard of all this evil that was come upon him, they came every one from their own place— JOB 2:11.
Their travel would have taken time.
Job must have walked in Uz after his disasters fell— and heard the young men deride him— to which he replies throughout the 30th chapter—
They abhor me, they flee from me— and spare not to spit in my face.
Because he has loosed my cord, and afflicted me, they have also let loose their bridle before me.
They came upon me as a wide breaking in of waters; in the desolation they rolled themselves upon me.
Terrors are turned upon me; they pursue my soul like the wind, and my welfare passes away like a cloud.
And now my soul is poured out upon me; the days of affliction have taken hold upon me.
My bones are pierced in me in the night season; and my sinews take no rest.
By the great force of my disease is my garment changed; it bindeth me about like the collar of my coat— JOB 30:10–18.

I am searching for footing in this look into the Book of Job. This search for grounding. The uncovering of frightful thoughts from which there is possibly something to learn. The certainty of the daysman-to-come in God's world— against the intrusion of otherness that works to diminish the meaning of the cross— which is a plank over the quicksand. It all seems a battle-zone as I think on the Book of Job.

There are dangers in possibilities. The attack of possibilities until the reader also is in the mire with the flags and the flagging Job.
The dangers of imaginative thought. The necessity of conjecture. Interpretation. What does this mean? How many meanings can it mean?

My shortcomings are ever before me. My sins, I think God would call them. I am called by the gravity of my situation. The graveness of my position before God. I need to know my limitations— I need to know I am not the captain of Uz.

Take away the dross from the silver, and there shall come forth a vessel for the refiner— PROVERBS 25:4. There are questions that come with that verse. As the refining pot for silver, and the furnace for gold, so is man to his praise— PROVERBS 27:21. And how does a man praise when his throat is closed off with rage? And what does that proverb mean? What multiple interpretations are possible— Suffering is a refining pot? Whatever is in the metal rises to the surface as it is heated? As a man praises God, bitterness rises to his mind the way dross rises from silver in a refining pot? Or does it mean, As a man is praised, pride can rise?— as happened in Job's earlier life when he walked in the streets and sat in the gate as the Earl of Uz.

If a man praises, and is not feeling praise, the truth will rise.

Actually, it's the interstices that rise—
the interpolations
containments
coalescences
exploitations

The singed pasture where 7,000 sheep burned— that remains a field of mud when it rains. The sound of turning pages. The wife sniffing in all the regions of the hacienda. The house servants moaning the loss of the field servants. Job's own sniffings in the barren fields.

You thought it was different than it would be— but you are caught in what you feared.

Then let my arm fall from my shoulder blade, and my arm be broken from the bone— JOB 31:22.

For destruction from God was a terror to me, and by reason of his brightness I could not endure— JOB 31:23.

Yes, it is his light I feel. The problem is— it makes ashes of my bones. I am nothing before him. The noble Job comes to nothing in the face of the grace of God. I feared what I didn't understand. What I didn't want to happen. What I dreaded would happen. He took what I knew and confronted me with the unknown. I feared what I didn't understand— his betrayal.

JOB IN THE INTERSTICE III

What does God want?— total prostration never to rise again?— awareness of the ant's breath I am in God's great universe?

Who can say to God, What are you doing?— JOB 9:12. And haven't you done it long enough?

Whatever is on the front line of his war, I wasn't ready for it yet. I was running and he took my feet. He slowed me to a crawl. To a stop. Forever, it seemed. Before there would be restoration. I believe God. I believe the spirit of him on the land. Nosing into every ditch. Upturning every stone. I want to remind God of his benevolence in his siege.

The stones of the field may be in league with him, but I feel them thrown at me.

In this new time— there was an age before this— maybe even ages before this. God tells us little— but there is evidence in the layers of the earth— maybe there have been ages upon ages. But for now, we are jostled in his croquet game— 4,000 years in the Old Testament. 2,000 since the New Testament. We are the wooden ball hit with a mallet through a wire wicket.

We balance the relationship of what is not known to what is experienced. As we are set in mystery to see what can be known and lived with what cannot be known. And to feel how grace meets the croquet mallet on the ball of our head— the boils erupting on our body.

Let him take his rod away from me, and let not his fear terrify me—
JOB 9:34.

If our dichotomy could be bearable, which it is not— we see why God showed Job the troubled waters. The Uz River— drybed at most. But in a sudden rain— a storm— a deluge for a morning, it overflows into Uz. And Job speaks in council of drainage. How to build a little canal— a ductwork that would score the runoff and keep it out of town.

I cry unto you and you do not hear. I stand up and you regard me not.
You become cruel to me: with your strong hand you oppose yourself against me.
I know that you will bring me to death, and to the house appointed for all the living.
Did I not weep for the troubled? Was I not grieved for the poor?
I looked for good, but evil came. I waited for light, but there was darkness.
My bowels boiled and rested not, the days of affliction came upon me.
I am a brother to dragons, and companion to owls— from JOB 30:20–29.

Have I seen any perish for want of clothing?— JOB 31:19. My wife and her sewing club provided for them.

That which I feared has come upon me. The boils have set me on fire?— no. The talkative friends I would behead if I could?— no. The loss of children?— yes— in part— for I am now without heirs.

Listen to my diatribe. What anger buried in the righteous Job. What blunderbuss.

Where shall wisdom be found?— JOB 28:12.
[The fear of the Lord, that is wisdom; and to depart from evil is under-standing— JOB 28:28]

The sea is not with me. Where is the water of understanding?

There is no island of the innocent.

JOB IN THE INTERSTICE IV

Then the Lord answered Job out of the whirlwind and said— JOB 38:1.

How did the Lord speak? Was he a disembodied voice? What did his voice sound like?

He spoke in the whirlwind. [The same whirlwind that caused the house to fall upon his sons and daughters— JOB 1:18–19.]

In Exodus 19:16, there also was thunder and lightnings and thick clouds on the mount that hid God [mainly to protect the people who would perish if they saw him]. But God spoke to Moses with a voice— EXODUS 19:19.

There are a lot of places in the Bible where the Lord spoke directly to his people and they heard his voice— Moses, Abraham, Samuel, David, the prophets— all of them the Lord spoke to— they heard and understood.

Maybe the Lord still speaks to us in prophecy in the voices of others. Maybe he mostly speaks in the words of Scripture.

The voices of Job's friends also served God's purpose. Along with the sufferings allowed by God, the accusations of Job's friends drove Job to a new understanding that God desired. Their arguments grounded Job in his persistence that God was just despite thoughts to the contrary. Job departed from his own reasoning— and became entrenched in his faith in God no matter the circumstances. He suffered the shaking of all he knew, until that which could not be shaken remained— HEBREWS 12:27.

Maybe Job wandered the fields and pens of his hacienda, crying out to God. Maybe he sat at the little caves along the escarpment on the edge of his land near the tomb where the bodies of his sons and daughters were kept. Maybe sometimes the dogs that had guarded the flock followed him. Even they seemed to ask what had happened. They had nothing but the dirt clods to chase.

FLY SWATTER— MEAT CLEAVER— FOR THE STANDARD KITCHEN

A great wind came across the wilderness
and struck the four corners of the house— JOB 1:19

There *are* nights I believe they will come back—
For now the wild hawk flies— coyotes prowl.
On Coots Ranch Road a yellow Pontiac?
The lamb, the beaver— the wolverines howl.
Where are my ear muffs, my night goggles, my bed?—
There were seven sons and [yes] three daughters.
Their names on the escarpment with the dead—
Taken in a whirlwind to the otters—
The whales and badgers rule the universe.
The world is clattering with albatross.
A thousand fireflies confound— coerce
The fight of hope— and anger over loss.
Those creeping— flying devils in the dark—
On the road I see a headlight— a spark.

THEREFORE, THE WHERE WERE YOU? SPEECH OF JOB CHAPTERS 38–41 AFTER WHICH JOB REPENTS

She tans in a lounge chair
on the patio Job built in his better days.
"Job's wife brings coffee in the morning," JACLYN DWYER

Better days are on their way.
The stories of old floodmarks when an abundance of water covered—
JOB 22:16.
There is a drying again—
though the door sticks in dampness
the suffering begins to abate.

Boils dry up. New field servants hired.
Their families move in.
New children track mud into the house.
There is noise again.
How did he know the circuit of heaven if he had not walked there?—
JOB 22:14.

THE FIRST [OBSERVED] BLACK HOLE CYGNUS X-1. THE FIRST HEN [RAPHAELLA].

Wind in the stove vent rattled the chickens in the yard.
Quasars ate fuel until expended.
The coal bucket of the farmyard's black hole.
A troubled Job shining after his sorrows.
The farm Bible on the table.
Why not use the feathers?
A pillow for their bed.
Sheets from the wife's clothesline.
Wind blows in all that history from the past.
Plumage of the trees dropping their feathers in the yard.
Restoration of what was lost.
Eating all the nearby stars.

A MOLE IN UZ

Forgive us now this Job-like rant—
Maryann Corbett, "Prayer Concerning the New, More 'Accurate'
Translation of Certain Prayer"

She saw the everlasting glory of the Almighty's fire from which he
gathered animals who knew only darkness he took them to his
pastures they were pebbles in his hands his baggy trousers his flip-
flops on the floor of heaven he is a beast over-worn at times like us
a hacksaw in his hand he says he is with us his presence almost un-
noticed but he turns the burnt and sodden fields into tapestry he
knows how to restore the clematis leaves the elephant ears
where the Araucana of Job's wife hides her blue eggs her
life more ornate once the trouble passed.

PART EIGHT

RESTORATION

JOB'S WIFE

The Lord gave Job twice as much as he had before—
JOB 42:10—

1,000 yoke of oxen, 6,000 camels, 14,000 sheep, 1,000 asses
crowded in the fields and pastures.
What will Job do with all those animals?—
Who knew a blessing could be a burden?—
How will he feed double of all he had?
I was asleep when the whirlwind sucked our children up—
seven sons, three daughters. Lost. Lost and lost.
The son's house and household goods scattered across
the hacienda. What next? What next?— I wrote
in my book of sorrows. I keep a journal asking
God what he is doing. Once I start it's hard to stop.
I was expecting more boils on Job. More death—
more ever-ready friendly visits. But after them—
who was left— I ask you? Where is my broom?
My head? My battle ax? My buzz saw and hammer?
At least the Chaldeans and Sabeans stole the herds
of camels, ox, and asses— and left no messes.
Unlike the fire that burned up 7,000 sheep—
leaving bits of bone and tooth— clumps of charred wool.
The families of the dead field servants bereft.
The fire and the Chaldeans and Sabeans killed them, too.
The Lord gave Job twice as much as he had—

except the sons and daughters were not doubled.
The field servants would have to be replaced— somehow—
I write to God. There is no end of mourning.
The cost of loss in Job's daybook. His ledger.
He keeps numbers. I keep words.
I cannot hold them back like Job's friends spilling
at the mouth— a thousand yoke of thoughts.

AMERICAN VILLANELLE

*Terrance Hayes wrote "American Sonnet for My Past
and Future Assassin" published in* The New Yorker *and*
The Best American Poetry 2018 *without regular rhyme
and meter [but the volta is there].*

*I wanted to extend my study of the Book of Job into the
villanelle, with Jehorah's voice continuing in the circle
of her thoughts, though she was not American.*

The Lord gave Job twice as much as he had— JOB 42:10—
oxen, asses, camels, sheep— oxen, asses, camels, sheep—
What will he do with all those animals in the pen?

A thousand asses [gulp!]— Where will he keep them?
How did we reap this benefit from God?—[30]
The Lord gave Job twice as much as he had— JOB 42:10—

I can't believe!!— a blessing would become a burden.
Is there no hay fork in the field— no broom to sweep?
What will he do with all those animals in the pen?

[30] Here I had to depart from the expected rhyme

A thousand yoke of oxen is doubled again—
Without a leap our children restored in the same number.[31]
The Lord gave Job twice as much as he had— JOB 42:10.

The Sabeans and Chaldeans from the mountain
took oxen, asses, 6000 camels— but fire burned the sheep.
What will he do with all those animals in the pen?

I stood by the field and thought to write a letter then
to the Lord as I alone withstood the heap.
The Lord gave Job twice as much as he had— JOB 42:10—
What will he do with all those animals in the pen?

[31] ditto

ADDENDUM[32]

Dear Lord,

Is this it? I expected more over-wordy friends.
More trees blown down from the whirlwind
that took our children. You were on a roll—

Have you seen the pastures after servants burned
with 7,000 sheep?— These fragments
I write to you as inquiry. Lord— look at the

animals crowded in the field. Grumbling.
Grumbling every day. What will we do with
all of that? Is it possible for you to take back?

At least the friends made their muffled,
understated exit. Job changed after the trials
you allowed. He has enlarged his understanding
while I remain a bitter berry on your vine.

Signed,
Jehora, Job's wife

---

[32] The villanelle could not contain the content, but spilled across the border onto another
page, and wanted to be called villanelle also.

TRAVEL FROM PITTSBURGH [AGAIN]

WRITING THE VERSIONS: A RECURRENCE OF VARIATION

Living as we do in a broken world, essays are bound to become more broken, fragmented— HILTON ALS, *Introduction,* The Best American Essays 2018

1.

January 11–12, 2019, in a Midwest snowstorm, I drove 840 miles from Pittsburgh to Kansas City in 17 hours. East of Effingham, Illinois, I saw a haze that was the beginning of the snow. It continued to snow until I reached my house in Kansas. I don't often drive that long at one time. But it was too hard to get off the road. I stopped for gas up snow-packed exit ramps, and that was it. 40 miles an hour for the last 250 miles across Missouri— St. Louis west to Kansas City. I couldn't see the line on the highway because the road was covered with snow. But the warning grooves at the side of the road growled if I got on them. I felt I was driving in the sky. There were times I felt my car leave the road where another world moved. I could not do much else than keep my hands on the circle of wheel in the geometry of driving.

2.

Driving in snow at night. The stars and moon had fallen from the cliff of the sky. The snow was their shattering. Their flakes covered the highway. It was as if it was in the beginning when people walked in darkness. The trees bowed under the weight of snow and the knowledge they carried fragments of the moon and stars on their back. The people made their way along the long trail of the road. There would be no light in the night sky but the people kept moving.

The earth itself moved forward even when it passed the same places it already had been. If only it could be made to know it was oblivious to the surroundings on its circuitous path around the sun.

On a long drive over the road a driver kept driving and snow kept falling and the car kept moving into a country of suspension the driver hadn't known was there. Until it was. All night the driver continued through the unknown knowing then it was there— when the weight of migration pushed the people onward in the remains of what was left. And the car kept following the tunnel of its headlights in the recurrence of a winter storm.

3.

Porism— In ancient mathematics a proposition that uncovers the possibility of finding such conditions as to make a specific problem capable of innumerable solutions.
Webster's New World Dictionary of the American Language, College Edition, 1966

4.

A re-version of the journey—

January 11, 2019, I left Pittsburgh after my last class at Carlow University in a low-residency MFA program. The morning classes were over at noon. I didn't stay for the rest of the day, but drove from downtown Pittsburgh to 376 west along the Allegheny River to 79 south to I-70 west at Washington, Pennsylvania, across a narrow slice of West Virginia into Ohio, Indiana, Illinois, Missouri, the border of Kansas. It was a road I was familiar with. I had driven it before. More than once before. By 5:00 p.m. in Illinois it was dark. East of Effingham I saw a haze in the headlights of the eastbound lane. It was snow. It was still snowing when I reached Kansas City at 5:00 a.m. the next morning, January 12. I drove over the road with the slow patience of Job. Exit ramps were filled with snow— with a ridge to get across if a snowplow had passed. I got off only for gasoline. The snow coming toward the car was a circle of orbiting stars. Snow fell steady on I-70. Sometimes it sounded like sleet. Sometimes a brief respite. But it continued to snow. I crossed the bridge across the Mississippi and Missouri Rivers at St. Louis. The Missouri River again at Booneville midway across the state. The limestone bluffs were white walls. It was a closed-in world. A terrain of white. Trucks and a few cars passed. A small caravan of Job's camels from Uz. Some in the ditch ahead. The snow covered lane markers. I recognized the buzz of tires in the warning grooves at the edge of the road and the driver got back on the road. Slowly. And more slowly. 250 miles across Missouri at 40 miles an hour. Sometimes less. Never more. It was a time of cold and darkness yet the snow was lit as if by a dim night-light. It was a time of slow momentum when the old world showed itself. I continued into the snow as though knowing always it was there to be taken to be used when the world I knew came to an end as maybe at the end of life when the driving was driving home.

5.

The old ones traveled with the car. I followed them through the snow. I knew they were with me. They were the car. The snow. The way through the snow. I heard their old stories in the voice of the snow. The brokenness held together with stories. They called the snow to hide the animal behind the storm. A terrapin walked with it. The storm was an old being. Many had walked in it. The cold is a predator. It stalks its prey. Biting first the toes. The fingers. Then working its way to the heart. The car is a hunter. The car is a spirit. I am the car that continues on the road. It is the old ones holding the car there. The car is an island in a white sea. The car is old migration trails. It is a sledge— not a hammer but sleigh or sled moving through the snow. How often words are at war with themselves carrying meanings that have nothing to do with one another. How often the car leaves the road and connects with old journeys. How often one meaning becomes many.

Over the snowy terrain now frozen into sleet pecking at the windshield trying to get into the car— asking for a ride— just one ride to warmer landscape— out of the ten to eleven inches on the backside of the storm.

A highway is a book of many versions. A highway is a book of many warnings.

Beware of hostiles in the atmosphere. Tell the snow its whiteness will tarnish. The road does not stay white for long. The snow turns brown with passing traffic.

In snow and the unraveling of steady travel the *woo woo* bands at the edge of the road—the shoulder rumble-strips warn to get back on the road. The animal behind the snow will get you.

6.

A few days later, I am driving again. This time in Texas, without the storm. At one point the highway made a curve. Almost before I knew it, I was in the inside lane headed for the edge of the road, but was able to turn the car back to the road. How easy to leave the road in an instant— to let the car go its own way in the momentum of forward travel. To relinquish movement— to turn— to guide— to steer. As if it was not an animal on the open range, but something I had to do to stay on the road.

I have a small house in Kansas. A smaller place in Texas. On my son's property in the country just south of the Red River. In a Butler building. In a part of the barn that is a Butler building. I travel back and forth between Kansas and Texas. The 482-mile trip takes 7½ hours. I stop halfway at a Mexican restaurant in Blackwell, Oklahoma.

7.

A few nights later, January 20–21, 2019, there was a blood wolf moon. It was a backlit maroon like the snow at night I drove through in the dim night-light from the other room. The blood moon reflects the earth's umbra— the sunsets and sunrisings that culminate around the earth. Our shadow is a dark red haze. As if the earth was a slow-burning ball of peat. In the wide sky above Texas anyway.

8.

The mathematical term, porism, transposes to writing. Because I asked it to. It is the stories the old ones tell as they travel. They unravel a story. They cover it with snow. The early people told stories to lessen the hold of their circumstances. Later travelers in the snow could hear it— if they knew to listen.

Language is both the creator and the world it creates. Language is the revealer and the revealed.

As the word made flesh— John 1:14— Jesus the creator and the world his words created— the preacher in a fundamental church in Texas would say. As language makes the world and is the world it makes.

9.

I am interested in the arrangement of shapes. Especially the forms of thought. A solid geometry of sorts.

Euclid described properties of the square car, the round earth, the line of the road, the point of the meteor that hit the blood wolf moon during the eclipse. The driver deduced the round head, the needful line of vision, the blunt point of impact if the car would hit.

Einstein's theory of relativity offers Euclidean geometry abundance and breakage from restraint. Therefore, other possibilities than impact appear on the highway.

Porism offers the possibility of finding such conditions as will render certain problems intermediate, or capable of innumerable solutions. The car will stay on the road. The driver will drive without sleep. There is a way through the storm if the driver continues.

But the definition is slightly inaccurate because the proposition actually states the conditions rather than affirming the possibility of finding them— Porism is a mathematical proposition or corollary, in particular the term porism has been used to refer to a direct result of a proof, analogous to how a corollary refers to a direct theorem— Wikipedia.

Nonetheless, the driver discovers supposition and the slippage of possibilities in porism as the structure of the world in which the driver drives.

The driver likes the oppositions in the ancient use of porism. Possibilities can be both. Neither. Or parts in one of both. Further, if not in actuality. In theory at least.

In the end, the innumerable solutions of porism reduce to one— keep driving— even at a terrapin pace.

10.

[At times] I could not discern the form thereof— JOB 4:16. Therefore, the driver kept driving through the hours of the night from Pittsburgh to Kansas.

The driver could not cross the Missouri River in Missouri without thinking of the 1804–06 Lewis & Clark Expedition, which the driver researched in the past. L&C mostly *drove* west to find place, to name and claim what they found— creeks, rivers, mountain ranges, plains. Their journey just as tenuous. Actually more so. Without interstate and bridges to help across. Without enclosure of car to protect from.

Past travels are present in the present ones. The whole interstate an overlay of then and now. With the opposition also of stasis and momentum. The land moving. The land in place.

In travel, there is a *transfixation* of timespace in the variation of story.

Travel is a country of suspension in which the driver, the land and the travel across it become one. After all, porism is a relation that holds for an infinite range of values— but only if a certain condition is assumed— Wikipedia. It is possible to drive through snow moving on the road only if snow is there in the storm to drive through.

THE BAT HOUSE

And ah!

That I went to my star
Without bread.

From Here, FEDERICO GARCÍA LORCA, *translated by Sarah Arvio*

Those voices always have been with me. The belief I had minimal distance to the Cherokee heritage, but distance nonetheless.

There was otherness in my father's family. I have felt the others with me. I think I have seen them.

Native heritage is not always in categories. Native heritage is not always documented. There are loose hairs and strays.

I have been a controversial non-fit in both worlds. I have wanted to give up on trying to be in either one.

Some of it no more than chalk on the sidewalk as I drew a road where I was going to the place I went. I tell you of a long journey that is not yet over as it was not as yet for Lorca. Yet the blue cloth floating there. I have waited for the poplars to fall, but they have stayed awake.

Grandparents. Great-grandparents and back and back.

The writing process itself is my heritage. My trail through the swamp of the past. Truth in the turtle shell of variegated pattern. As a Christian truth for me is Christ, but not for others. After that truth is shattered into nimble only to hear what is told from various corners whatever terror is before it.

Some of it no more than chalk on the sidewalk as I found a road where I was going to the places I went. I tell you of a long journey that is not yet over. I have waited for the branches to fall but they stayed awake.

Blessed with books and classes and rocks picked up in travel and research. I'm grateful for gasoline. And the faces of sunflowers that follow the sun across the sky. There is a small sunflower in a chicken's eye. For Hannah, my trooper cat who traveled with me to Oklahoma, Iowa, Minnesota. In truth, I have been blessed by my Maker. The trembling woods. The poplars. I travel to my star without knowing who I am.

A DNA test European but for the Iberian peninsula with some contact the northern Africa. Research in Cherokee DNA has mideastern components. A heritage researcher who said that "The removal of the Cherokee from their lands east of the Mississippi River to Indian Territory did not include many Cherokee who had already purchased land and were established as part of European-American society. Over time these individuals and their descendants lost their identity as Native American. This can make documenting Cherokee heritage very difficult. So far, Woods Lewis and his family members have been identified as white in every U.S. census. However, there was no incentive to distinguish themselves as Native American on the census."

I like the Native American story of the bat that attended both councils of the birds and animals, and was looked at suspiciously by both. The bat is a mammal with wings. It is both and neither of both.

I have other travelers with me on the road. I think I have seen them. A portal in the dark as I wake. An image of some dim dawn-light with figures looking from. I don't know how else to say it. I don't know that it should be said. But others are with me.

I speak for the many who are undocumented. The unpapered Indian. Not Indian. A shadow-land. A marginal being. Not having a whole self but divided. With elisions. Lacuna.

Upside-down. The ceiling is the floor. The floor the ceiling. Pictures hang upside-down also. A bat dreams upside-down. A bat sleeps with his wings folded across his chest.

A bat defines gravity when it flies.

Without papers, one is a faux bat. French for fake. Bogus. Ersatz. A constructed narrative. Tropes tromps trimps.

There was otherness in my father's family. I have felt the others with me. I think I have seen them.

I am Fauxian Fauxesque. Indeterminate.

Using appropriations. I speak for the large tribe— the lost tribe of them. The poplars by the creek beyond the edge of the field. Or was it pasture?

From here— the inconclusive evidence— as I went to my star without bread.

UNICORN

Will the unicorn be willing to serve you, or abide by your crib?
Can you bind the unicorn with his band in the furrow? Or will he
harrow the valleys after you? Will you trust him, because his strength is
great? Or will you leave your labor to him? Will you believe him, that he
will bring home your seed, and gather it into your barn?— JOB 39:9-12

There is only mystery of *re'em*
the word translated unicorn
interpreted as wild ox
one-horned gnu
oryx or eland
ibex or gazelle.

re'em played hopscotch
chased peacock and hawk

sparked *millefleur* tapestry
of mythic horses
that young girls liked
trapezed on thought
desiring the uncertainty surrounding it all.

WRITING

Do you know how long it takes to find the way through the wilderness
following bread crumbs?
There are branchings in the road I could take out of there.
But I choose to go on— to wrestle with uncertainty.
A cold wind in the window I could shut.

Writing sounds close to righting and not lefting.
I could leave it with desire— but choose to write it on the page
until I can see what is there.
Do you know how many drafts come in that window—
one after another?

Language is a buffalo herd larger and more numerous than me.
Fierce. Grunting.
I am fighting a buffalo herd with a bow and arrow when I write.
I have two legs, they have four— multiplied by a herd
until all I see are legs.
They are the wilderness I follow through—
pulling the drawstring of language.

I like the landscape of land.
The language that stretches like landscape on the road before me.
The rough weather. The distance.

I want to struggle.
I want to see what there is to write.

To see how it can be written.

I find failures and rewrites and rewrites rewritten

until my words are served on the page—

until my writing is curtains for that window I want always to leave

open.

JUMP SUIT

It's common as dirt, the story / of expulsion
Salt, LINDA GREGERSON

And Abimelech . . . beat down the city and sowed it with salt—
JUDGES 9:45

Scholars of narrative distinguish between fabula (what happens to the characters) and sujet (how and in what order a narrative shows these events).
The Poem Is You: 60 Contemporary American Poems and How to Read Them, STEPHANIE BURT

For want and famine they were solitary; fleeing into the wilderness in former time desolate and waste— JOB 30:3

This is what it was. After not knowing. But hearing fragments of what happened. And versions and reversions of those fragments.

I looked for her grave. Piecing together family history. Driving from Kansas to Moffett, Oklahoma, on the Fort Smith, Arkansas, border by the Arkansas River. Out in the country where dirt roads send a trail of dust. Arvezena Crawford Lewis, my great-great-grandmother, born in Tennessee. She went to Candy's Creek Mission School, established for Cherokee children by Dr. Samuel Worcester, a missionary to the Cherokee. She was there. My great-great-grandmother. With her spelling book and pencil, in her chair at a table writing letters of the alphabet that made words from her spelling book. Her mother, Mary Waters Crawford. Her grandfather, Michael Waters, on the 1835 Cherokee census.

After the 1838–39 Removal of the Cherokee— after resettlement had settled, the family also went to Indian Territory. Arvezena had by then a son-in-law, John Kesterson, a white man, who was told by a so-called Indian agent that they could go and settle there. Kesterson went to Cherokee County first and farmed a piece of land, slow as pork, but settled nonetheless and tried to get on the rolls as a Cherokee citizen because of his wife, but was rejected. Arvezena went to Indian Territory in 1887, several years after her son-in-law, Kesterson. Arvezena's sons and their families also were there. Maybe it was after Arvezena's husband, David Lewis, died. But they were rejected despite all the layers that lawyers in Fort Smith could do. It seems John Kesterson irritated some of the Cherokee agents the way he insisted on Cherokee membership, though he was not Cherokee, but was married to one and was there to partake of the benefits that the agent in Tennessee told him he would receive.

Arvezena Crawford Lewis, my great-great-grandmother, and her family, including a son, Jonathan Woodson Lewis—Woods Lewis— my great- grandfather, were thrown out on the road with John Kesterson in Cherokee County, and lived in the woods with a few boards over them.

John Welch, the Indian agent, told them because Arvezena was in Candy's Creek Mission School for Cherokee children, if they moved to Indian Territory they could enroll as Cherokee and receive land.

Maybe the agent wanted their land in Tennessee. Who knows who he was. The family tried for seven years to enroll. They were rejected and finally removed by those who had been removed. Arvezena Lewis remained in Indian Territory with some of her family and moved to Sequoyah County. She is buried in Paw Paw Cemetery on the eastern edge of Oklahoma. The place of paw paws, a little runt of a tree with the shoats of its fruit sucking its teats.

There were other reasons the family was not liked— though they remain mysterious. Woods Lewis, my great-grandfather, a brother-in-law to Kesterson, had an injury to his hand. A burn injury. Someone said from taking an iron from the fire to strike. To hurt. To maim, and was himself burned in his hand, after which he fled to Arkansas. They all must have been scrappy. My father, Lewis Hall, carried a scar on his hand between his thumb and first finger in that place— the thenar— like the flat shore between a bend in the river. Myself with burn scars on my legs when I knelt down on a floor furnace as a child to see the fire that burned below. A camp fire in the woods where my great-great grandmother sat removed from her house and possessions. It was the same fire that burned in the floor furnace of the grocers on the corner of the street in Kansas City where I lived. This is the which to which I belong. Dispossessed of heritage. More than a table and chairs. A chest of drawers. A few beds. Their rickety frames easily broken when thrown from a house. A small child didn't know the grate over the floor furnace would burn through coat and leggings to the legs— as fire always seeks the bones. Those burn scars with specked skin that look like toad skin that covers the bones in the legs or hands of father and great grandfather.

The directions to Paw Paw Cemetery near Moffett, Oklahoma, where

Arvezena Lewis is buried, is difficult as the past. I tell you none of it is easy. There was a family of European descent that by marriage thought they would be recognized as Cherokee and were not. They plotted to be accepted with testimony of someone who had known Arvezena at Candy's Creek, it being a school where mostly Cherokee went. But she was not recorded anywhere as Cherokee as the family was remiss in letting their heritage matter until they thought there was something in it for them. Opportunity was the word. In the hot afternoon between cornfields and dirt roads that went one way and another over drainage ditches and creeks past water wheels and irrigation pumps that brought up water from underground where Arvezena rests in Paw Paw Cemetery.

The directions to the cemetery take most of a page. I got lost several times and gave up until I saw two men in pickups talking at the intersection of Highway 64 just south of I-40— and one of them led me to the cemetery.

HOW TO GET TO PAW PAW CEMETERY IN SEQUOYAH COUNTY, OKLA-HOMA, NEAR FORT SMITH, ARKANSAS: Apparently no one has an actual map of the area showing all roads, especially since names were replaced with numbers for roads. But if you will carefully follow these instructions, in order, it should not be difficult. (I don't know how it is after a lot of rain, on these dirt and gravel roads.) If you are at the west end of the bridge from Fort Smith, Arkansas, on Highway 64 (east–west), it will be nine and one-tenth miles after the turn-off ramp (off of Highway 64 into Moffett, Oklahoma) to Paw Paw Cemetery southwest of Moffett. That is, by these directions. Most of it is a maze out there, through farm land, with dirt and gravel roads. So do it right the first time and you might save a lot of time and not be left wandering the maze which includes dead-end roads. Start counting distance when you leave the ramp into Moffett. All distance readings I give you will mean the distance from this ramp. Leaving the ramp into Moffett, just follow the main little paved road south a little way, and it will curve west. At one-half mile, you will see the Moffett City Hall and Police Department on your right. Keep going west. It will become Old Highway 64. Keep going west. At three and six-tenths miles (remember, from the Moffett ramp) you will see a darkish-green metal building on your right with small print on the side facing the highway, showing: "Sheffield Farms." Turn left (south) onto the dirt road with a little street sign that says: S 4790 Rd. Keep going south until your total distance traveled (from the Moffett ramp) is four and eight-tenths miles. Here, the road makes a little jag to the right, crossing a tiled drainage-way and back toward south. At five and seven-tenths miles, you come to a fence and have to turn right (west). At six and two-tenths miles, you have to turn left (south) and your road (S 4790 Rd) becomes S 4785 Rd. At six and six-tenths miles, there is a jag to the right toward several items of metal equipment, and a jag back toward south. At seven and three-tenths miles, go until you get to the left–right (east–west) road (NOT the one that turns right just before you get there). You can see (but don't turn) that within sight the road going left (east) quickly curves around toward the south. So, you will know you have come right so far. But turn RIGHT. At seven and seven-tenths miles, DON'T PASS UP S 4780 Rd on your left. Turn left (south), with a fence on your left. Keep going south until your total miles from the Moffett ramp is almost NINE miles. Watch for the little white rectangular sign on your left that says: Paw Paw Cemetery. A road turns left (east), and you already see that less than one-tenth mile out there is a cemetery, at the edge of the woods.

In records, her name spelled several ways. Arvezena, Arvizena, Arvezenia, Arajine, Arizona, and Arvazein on her gravestone. As if letters were not made clearly as taught in Candy's Creek Mission School for Cherokee children. But census and roll takers sometimes were careless in writing the names they heard.

My great grandfather, Woods Lewis, named his daughter, Orvezene, after his mother, Arvezena. Did my grandmother, Orvezene, have burn scars also— like her grandfather, father and granddaughter? I hardly saw her. She died when I was eleven. She lived in Arkansas and we in Missouri.

Family history is a little herd of pigs.

No more than a speck in the sky, as if someone jumped from a plane.

They would have sold pig milk if they could.

But family history is unfinished business, as it is called. I knew I had Cherokee blood, but the source farther back than I knew.

My paternal family members were intruders in Cherokee County. Evict the Lewis-Kesterson family by force, which they did May 23, 1888.

They were driven forth from among men (they cried after them as after a thief)— JOB 30:5

It was John Kesterson who wrote— Now on May 23 two days after the sale of my home and the very day when I and my family were driven at the muzzles of Winchester rifles and revolvers from my house my household goods and provisions thrown into the road and my aged and sick mother-in-law (though Arvezena lived another 22 years) compelled to leave her bed for the shelterless forest.

They moved from Cherokee County south to Sequoyah County, still in Indian Territory.

In the trial, an affidavit of Thomas J. Taylor stated, when Arvezena was a girl about 10 years old she was put in school Candy's Creek, Tennessee. My brother James and two of my sisters were boarding at the school at the time, and I was a day schooler. She derives her Cherokee blood from her mother, whose maiden name was Waters. I last saw her in 1831 at Chattanooga, Tennessee. Her father was John Crawford, a white man and her mother and grandfather were Cherokee. Her father, John Crawford, ran Blair's Ferry close to Red Clay, Georgia. Yet in 1881, 50 years later, he still knew her. A story floating on the river without a paddle.

But Arvezena was never enrolled as Cherokee. Possibly her father, John Crawford, did not want his wife, Mary Waters, or his children recognized as Cherokee. He ran Blair's Ferry to get horse and wagon across the water, to take from here to there. To go. To jump from land to water to land again. It's what you get when you don't enroll properly as though it mattered. And generations later there's still the same call to Cherokee as an outsider. A hanger on.

Though Arvezena was sent to a national school for Cherokee children and was known as Cherokee. She was the daughter of Mary Waters and granddaughter of Michael (Michell) Waters, whose name is on the 1835 Cherokee roll as a resident of Candy's Creek, Tennessee. Mark Lewis, another son of Arvezena Lewis, is on the 1910 Cherokee rolls. So there. Sotheresothere. We are still here. Saying much the same.

The Lewis-Kesterson family did not arrive in Indian Territory on the Removal Trail but came forty years later mixed with white members of the family over several years in the early 1880s, and thought they could sign up, be accepted, farm a parcel of land. And by 1887 were declared intruders and removed from their farm.

The 1835 Cherokee rolls listed persons in the household, but nothing more than the man's name, the head of the household.

Males under 18	3	
Males over 18	1	Michael (Michell) Waters
Females under 16	2	
Females over 16	1	his unnamed wife
Total Cherokees	7	
Farms	1	
Acres in Cultivation	13	

The Family Research Center at the Cherokee National Museum in Tahlequah, Oklahoma, printed 123 pages of the family's legal struggles for recognition. They are full of letters from lawyers, letters signed by notary publics, testimonies, affidavits, summons, court decisions, appeals, protests, pig squeals, haranguing. They involve the Adair Court, which was the new Office of Commission on Citizenship, the Sheriff of the Sequoyah District of the Cherokee Nation, the United States Court for the Indian Territory, Northern Judicial Division, Muskogee, Indian Territory, the Commissioner of the Office of Indian Affairs, Secretary of the Department of the Interior, Washington, D.C., the Supreme Court.

The United States finally issued a ruling on December 21, 1897 against the plaintiffs / claimants. The opinion says, in part, Although the proof is somewhat vague and undefined, there seems to be sufficient proof to justify us in holding that the claimants are persons of Cherokee blood and that Arizona Lewis, the principal claimant, was so recognized by the State of Tennessee, where she resided prior to coming to the Cherokee Nation in 1887.

Still, in conclusion, the United States court upheld the Adair Court decision from 10 years prior indicating insufficient proof existed to claim membership in the Cherokee Nation. Indian Territory had the jurisdiction. The decision was theirs.

Though they lacked authority to seize, confiscate, and sell the belongings of a non-Cherokee citizen of the U.S., John Kesterson ordered the Cherokee Nation to make an additional payment for the value of property that had been seized and sold years ago.

It is not known if payment was made.

But Kesterson paid no rent for seven years, the Cherokee authorities said.

I knew all this after paying a researcher at Legacy Tree in Salt Lake City— and after DNA testing led me to relatives in Arkansas I didn't know I had. One of them, Jeff Lewis, had done extensive research. I corroborated his information at the Cherokee Family Research Center in the Cherokee Heritage Museum in Tahlequah, Oklahoma, and received a certificate—

The Cherokee National Historical Society, Inc. recognizes Diane Glancy as a Life Member of the heraldic organization First Families of the Cherokee Nation. This certificate does not infer or imply eligibility for citizenship for the recipient in any federally recognized Cherokee tribe or nation nor does it grant the recipient the necessary credentials to pursue state or federal recognition. It does recognize the recipient as a direct descendant of Michael Waters and their connection with the historic Cherokee nation on or before 6 September 1839. Signed Shane Jett, President, Cherokee National Historical Society. August 25, 2018. Member #1255.

It was then the sky moved from the earth with a plane rising on it. I was mostly European— a person of minimal Cherokee blood but not a member of the Cherokee Nation— now jumped from the plane no longer claiming more heritage than I have. The ferry not river now but plane. To go from land to sky to land again. The grumbling in the fields at pumping stations— as if a little nest of pigs in jump suits returned to roads between the cornfields of earth.

WHERE IS THE IS THAT IS IS?

The *island of the innocent* was spoken by Eliphaz— one of the Job friends— who came to Uz huffed with his own thoughts— The righteous do not suffer. Though it was established that Job was a righteous man, and that Job was suffering. Therefore, Eliphaz had to reason through the contradiction he faced. He concluded that Job was suffering because Job had sinned. Further, Eliphaz the Temanite, knew how alleviate suffering, and that was doing right-doing instead of wrong-doing. Job should confess his sin, withdraw from it, and God would remove Job's suffering from Job. Further, Job would dwell once again on the island of the innocent— with Eliphaz, Bildad, Zophar, and now Elihu, the fourth friend. There were other inhabitants of the island located somewhere in the great sea of the innocent where no one suffered because they were innocent and God did not let them suffer because they had done nothing wrong. It is the innocence of conscience of which Eliphaz, Bildad, Zophar and Elihu were owners— Yet Job knew in his misery, there-was-nothing-he-could-do-it-was-in-God's-hands. That's who had the clean hands. And the island of the innocent belonged to God alone. Possibly, no one else lived there. On earth, there is none righteous, no, not one— ROMANS 3:10. There is none that doeth good, no, not one— PSALM 14:3. There is not a just man on earth that doeth good and sinneth not— Ecclesiastes 7:20. Though there is contradiction— Noah was a just man and perfect in his generation— GENESIS 6:9. As Job, Abraham, David, and others were also called righteous.

Job met with friends in their meeting that seemed it would never end. Until God spoke and talked through four chapters of the Book of Job and made himself clear. And then continued in an end chapter when God asked Job to pray for his friends and he would forgive them for pushing on the suffering Job more suffering with their words that were not right— JOB 42:7. And the friends returned to their land from which they came having their ideas shuffled, that opened a can of possibilities, which was what Job feared in the first place. The adjustments. Whew. The adjustments. The earth was a place for adjustments. As God's kingdom was a kingdom of corrections.

Job's prosperity was restored and he had to go restored into the messy world of conflicting realities where he had, in stubbornness, stuck with faith no matter what, even when wondering where was home base after all?

Was it nothing but a long journey of turnings on an over-dusty road full of voices saying this-is-the-way though no one knew what was on the other side of the Great Mystery but maybe Mystery itself was on a journey as they were on a journey trying to figure out which voices on the road were going in the right direction? In the meantime they walked in the mystery of the journey in which many voices on the road said many different things about the Great Mystery that was ahead where the One Old, the Great One who was a trickster, it seemed, let his people wander with major adjustments from time to time. From which the three friends and the fourth, Elihu, corrected somewhat, traveled on, considering still whether to be bold or not bold, to speak or not speak, as they made their way through their thoughts— and maybe they were sorry for their trip to Job's hacienda, yet grateful nonetheless for the forgiveness they received and that's the last time they would travel so far to offer help. Though the first inclinations would show up to do battle with again and again. And all the voices— all the diversity— all the redundancies of the choruses that called one aside or stirred the dust or blurred the vision— as the earth was a place of dust that called them ahead on what each believed to be their journey on the right path.

And the Old One on his throne over the earth looked down at the free-wheeling people he made from ape, from dirt, from his breath— and what Zip Code did he reside in, after all? Why so distant, God— that you let people stumble around in the darkness they found to stumble around in?

Maybe God himself is turning on a journey in the benefit of possibilities as he creates the Great Mystery on the road of his own direction—

NOTES

If I covered my sins as Adam— JOB 31:33

"History (2) by Interlocutory" was taken from John James's poem, "History (n.)," published in *The Kenyon Review* and *The Best American Poetry 2017*. In the backnotes of the *Contributors' Notes and Comments*, Jones writes, *I was experimenting at the time with spacing and alignment, as well as with the short, fragmented sections that comprise the poem.*

After reading the poem, I wanted to write words. I wanted to read words. I wanted to learn how others write. I wanted to write words until a landscape began to form. I wanted to rock words in my chair. Sometimes a few lines appeared on my paper. They were the beginning of structure. A house is a poem. A place of habitation where thoughts are kept. Sorted. Arranged. Ordered. Sometimes disordered—

But often poetry is more about the scattering than it is the appropriation. The new brokenness of the broken world. The modernity of the bricolage, though it always has been with us. The stepped-up coercion of a single meaning— now decentered— that lets the vehicle run on various highways at once— a vehicle dispensing an array of slippages and tautologies. The derailments of the author's voice from text, and text from subtext. What containment or constrainment holds the bricolage on track? To dissonate. Or is it detonate? The borrowing and being influenced by.

The Book of Job is about suffering. It is about patience during that suffering. There is nothing Job can do but wait. What will God do? Will suffering continue? What is left for Job to lose? His sons and daughters are dead. The flocks and herds of his fields and pastures have been taken by fire and marauders. Boils cover Job's body. His wife keeps her distance after the response she is known for— curse God and die. Job's three friends show up. They offer no consolation, but ask Job what he's done to receive the wrath of God. There is discourse of trial and tribulation. A fourth man arrives to say the same as the three. There are spots of promise in one or two places— I know if I die, I will see God. But Job does not die— at least not then. Finally, God speaks to the five men, which must have been horrific. Job discovers humility, and repents of his arrogance in the face of God. In the end, there is reparation for Job— more than restoration. But what is in the story of the story of Job— as if that was not enough? And what of the story of that story's story?

I think of David in the Psalms when I read the Book of Job. There is the same passion. The same overwrought expression. The same artistic imagination. The same determined faith. Even some of the same wording. If the Book of Job is an accumulation of several voices telling an old story of the suffering of the upright, David may have had a hand. There seems to be a strong link between David and the Book of Job.

There came a great wind from the wilderness— JOB 1:19
He shall take them away as with a whirlwind— PSALM 58:9

Let that day be darkness, let not God regard it from above, neither let the light shine upon it— JOB 3:4
Like the untimely birth of a woman, that they may not see the sun— PSALM 58:8

Happy is the man whom God correcteth— JOB 5:17
Blessed is the man whom thou chastenest— PSALM 94:12

What is man that you should magnify him, and that you should set your heart upon him . . . and visit him?— JOB 7:17–18
What is man that you are mindful of him? And the son of man, that you visit him?— PSALM 8:4

Before I go to the place from which I shall not return, even to the land of darkness and the shadow of death— JOB 10:21
Though I walk through the valley of the shadow of death— PSALM 23:4

He pours contempt on princes— JOB 12:21
He pours contempt on princes— PSALM 107:40

And though after my skin worms destroy this body, yet in my flesh shall I see God— JOB 19:26
God will redeem my soul from the power of the grave: for he shall receive me— PSALM 49:15

JOB 21:7–11 and PSALM 73:3–11 on the prosperity of the wicked

He delivers the innocent man, you will be delivered through the cleanness of your hands— JOB 22:30
Who shall ascend into the hill of the Lord? Or who shall stand in his holy place? He that has clean hands— PSALM 24:3–4

I broke the jaws of the wicked, and plucked the spoil out of his teeth— JOB 29:17
I went out after him, and smote him, and delivered it out of his mouth— I SAMUEL 17:35
[David speaking of the lion and bear that took a lamb from the flock]

Then the Lord answered Job out of the whirlwind and said— JOB 38:1
I answered you in the secret place of thunder— PSALM 81:7

In A.D. 391, not knowing where to put the Book of Job, but thinking it necessary, Jerome and the church fathers placed Job before Psalms, into which it spills anyway—

This could be Job speaking?—
How long wilt thou forget me, O Lord? Forever? How long wilt thou hide thy face from me? How long shall I take counsel in my soul, having sorrow in my heart daily? How long shall mine enemy be exalted over me? Consider and hear me, O Lord, my God, lighten mine eyes, lest I sleep the sleep of death—
PSALM 13:1–3

Maybe there are original parts of the story, and parts written later— the beginning, the end, the visit of the fourth friend, Elihu. What about God who seems full of questions and insecurities that make him want to prove himself to Satan, a fallen angel he created?

There is a Jobian terrain of uncertainty in the Psalms also. Psalm 38 could be the Psalm of Job— Your arrows stick fast in me, your hand presses me. There is no rest in my bones because of my sin. My wounds stink. I am troubled. Lord, my desire is before you, and my groaning is not hid from you.

The loss and agonies of Job— the confusion as to what has happened and why— the howlings of Job also are the howlings of the last of the Plains Indians. C.G. Jung and the Sioux Traditions, Vine Deloria, Jr.— "We are always caught between a vision or remembrance of a different kind of existence and the practical requirement of living in the flesh in a harsh and limited physical world."

On prairie nights, the tepees had a transparency from the firelight within. Pictographs on the tepee hides seemed to move in the flickering light. Smoke rising from the smoke holes made the tepees a village of small volcanoes. In the uncertainty of life, there was certainty in the cosmos in the structure and triangulation of the tepees— the tepee poles crossed toward the top to open again in the sky.

The story of the story of Job is that the believer is surrounded by a hedge— wherein are infinite possibilities for transformation and innumerable solutions for our sorrows.

ACKNOWLEDGMENTS

Aazhoomon Exhibition Catalogue, Miikanan Gallery of Native Art, Bemidji, Minnesota, for "Dressed in Trophy Clothes" from "The Long Arc of My Driving."

Across the Waves: Contemporary Poetry from Ireland and the United States, Jean O'Brien and Gerry La Femina, editors, Salmon Press, for "Chief Gull Recounts Greasy Grass on the Hill Where It Happened," third section in "Versions of the Many-Versions-of-Greasy-Grass," and "Driving through Snow across Ohio" with the comment, Sometimes I finish a poem and it continues. What I left out wants back into the poem where it feels it belongs. Maybe a poem that includes the left-out part could be called, *the iceberg construct*, to show the underwater part of a poem that is kept buried for the poem to remain poem and not prose.

Adam, Eve & the Riders of the Apocalypse, D.S. Martin, editor, Wipf & Stock, for "She Was the First to Speak" and "Comet-Man's Wife."

Beyond Baroque Literary Arts Center, Venice, California, for the 2019 first prize to "The first [observed] black hole Cygnus X-1. The first hen [Raphaella]" judged by Diane Seuss, who wrote, "The first [observed] black hole Cygnus X-1. The first hen [Raphaella]"— This poem is strange and sublime, approaching, in its unenjambed lines, an intersection between the first observed black hole and a hen—the wide expanse of the cosmos and the local particulars of a farm and its particular hen. The poem enacts this unlikely intersection via images and without overkill, rhetoric, or an over-conscious push toward meaning. In twelve lines, a magic both biblical and quotidian unfurls—even "the trees [drop] their feathers in the yard" as the black hole and the coal bucket eat "all the nearby stars."

Caliban #29 http://calibanonline.com/CO29/index.html October 2017 for "The So-Called Ostrich Speech," "He Have Nothing To Do the Rest of the Day but Jumping," and "An Ordinary Day to Work." For the contributor notes, I answered with the following— Larry Smith, thanks for taking these poems. It's a privilege to be included in *Caliban*. Acceptance always validates new work I am trying— a surreal study of the Book of Job— something I feel lurking under the surface. I am a weird Christian of sorts. I seem to see other moons circling the planets of the biblical texts— or some of them anyway. Plays on words or thoughts of stories that remain in memory mixed with childhood books that rhymed. There is an underbelly to it all. The unconscious mind has fun with biblical stories. It's the distillations and side-views that interest.

di-verse-city Anthology 2017, Austin International Poetry Festival, for "How Can I Keep from Happening This?"

Fifth Wednesday Journal, edited by Joan Murray, for "Butter Beans".

Jung Journal, Culture & Psyche for "I, Job."

Native Voices: Indigenous American Poetry, Craft and Conversation, edited by CMarie Fuhrman and Dean Rader, Tupelo Press, for "The Bat House," "He Dressed Me for the Pretend Cold" and "Until the times of restitution— ACTS 3:21."

Poetry Society of Pennsylvania Anthology for "Unicorn."

The Mockingbird for "With Dreams upon My Bed."

The Pittsburgh Current, 11/1/18 Tree of Life Synagogue Issue, Poetic Healing by Jody DiPerna, for "Where Does the River Go at Night?"

Whale Road Review for "Job, the Comet Man."

"An Act of Invasion," "More than Content Is the Manner in Which It Was Held" and "Jehorah" were read at the Center for Christian Thought, Biola University, March 29, 2018, in a program, *Poetry and Suffering*. Acknowledgment to Evan Rosa.

"Jump Suit" was read at the Native American Literature Symposium, March 7, 2019.

"The Long Arc of My Driving" was read at the University of Missouri, November 29, 2017.

Acknowledgment to Matthew Smith and *Christianity and Literature* for presenting the idea for "More than Content Is the Manner in Which It Was Held".

Gratefulness to Jan Beatty and the M.F.A. low-residency program at Carlow University in Pittsburgh, Pennsylvania.